Independent Schools' Guide 2025

Matthew Smith

Published in 2024 by Attain, an imprint of Chapel Studios Ltd
PO Box 1003, Oxford, OX1 9XG.

Copyright © Chapel Studios Ltd, 2024.

All rights reserved. No part of this publication may be reproduced, stored in a retrieval system, or transmitted, in any form or by any means, electronic, mechanical, photocopying, recording, or otherwise, without prior written permission from the copyright owner.

A CIP catalogue record for this book is available from the British Library.

Printed in the UK by CPI Group (UK) Ltd, Croydon, CR0 4YY.

ISBN: 978-1-7392041-0-5

1.0
For updates and changes, please visit:
attain.guide/updates

Attain and the Attain logo are registered trademarks of Chapel Studios.

Disclaimer: Independent education has a wide range of views and the use of quotations does not imply that these contributors share the same views as the author. The views and opinions of the author may also not necessarily be shared by all schools mentioned in this book. The author and publishers do not warrant, to the fullest extent permitted by applicable law, that the contents are error-free and shall not be liable for any loss, however arising, as a result of the information contained in this book.

Designed by Chapel Studios
chapelstudios.co.uk

To A and N,
with the hope I practise what I preach.

About the author
Matthew Smith is a journalist, writer and designer who has worked with the independent schools' sector for 25 years, advising clients on marketing, communications and strategy, and for 15 years as Editor of *Attain* magazine. Launched in 2006 to provide parents with a trusted guide to navigate the maze of independent schooling, he grew the title to become the leading magazine for the sector, with its content regularly featured by the national press. He is a Member of the Chartered Institute of Journalists and a Fellow of the Royal Geographical Society.

Attain Guide 2025

Contents

Before you begin

How this guide works	2
Starting the journey	6
Involving your child	10
Elephants in the room	13

Things to consider

The head	17
Pastoral care	21
Curriculum	25
Extracurricular	29

Things to avoid

Marketing spin	33
League tables	37
Unhelpful influences	41
Parental pressure	45

Practical aspects

Logistics	49
Inspection reports	53
Paying for it	56
Other considerations	59

Making decisions

Open days and admissions	63
Taking the long view	66

Schools' Directory	69

Attain Guide 2025

How this guide works

This book helps you make one of the hardest decisions you can take on behalf of your child. It deliberately doesn't tell you which private schools are the best in the country for exam success or rank the best for sport. It does not list the best headteachers nor frankly tell you 'the best' at anything.

What it does explain is why seeking out 'the best' for your child is one of the most unhelpful things you can do as a parent. It shows you where to focus your thoughts and what matters when evaluating different schools. You will see how marketing spin, league tables, awards and other unhelpful influences can get in the way. And it highlights the practical things which can make – or break – a choice of school. This book will tell you how to find the right school and be confident in that judgment.

By its very nature, education should be the process through which children have their eyes opened to the world. They get to see all the opportunities and possibilities which are available to them. Good teachers switch on light bulbs; they inspire and energise those in their care. This is vitally important in the primary years, when a child's thirst for knowledge is so strong. During this crucial time, your son or daughter will build the foundations from which to support all their subsequent learning – at senior school and beyond. Put simply, they will learn how to learn.

Before you begin

This book helps you make one of the hardest decisions you can take on behalf of your child. It deliberately doesn't tell you which private schools are the best in the country for exam success or rank the best for sport. It does not list the best headteachers nor frankly tell you 'the best' at anything.

This whole process has three partners: your child, the school and you. The trust you have in your child's school is a critical aspect in making it all work. It starts when you first choose the school and, like all relationships, you need to work at it by being active and engaged. During your child's journey through school, you will undoubtedly come across the occasional pothole in the road. Take the long view and trust in the school. Seek their advice and, above all, you need to remember why you chose it in the first place.

Let the school set the pace: weekends are for time together as a family, pursuing hobbies and interests. They are not for maths tutoring or an endless round of extra-curricular activities. Embrace the power of boredom. Your child (and the school) will thank you for it.

Nobody says it's easy being a parent. In most situations in life you use a combination of past experience and judgement to make a decision which, hopefully, turns out to be the right one. With schooling, past experience is a less useful ally as times have changed from when you set off each day, clutching a school bag. Some parents look back on their school days fondly and can easily critique the present as it doesn't match up to this rose-tinted nostalgia. Others have less favourable memories and this too can bring unhelpful comparisons.

> This whole process has three partners: your child, the school and you. The trust you have in your child's school is a critical aspect in making it all work.

Whether we like it or not, our time at school is unhelpful baggage. We have to accept that it is not relevant when helping our own children, except perhaps as a source of amusing anecdotes. But even here you have to be careful – telling your child funny tales of how you avoided doing much sport at school will hardly inspire them to Olympic greatness. But better this than the parent who wants their child to make the 1st XV where they didn't; vicariously going back to school to re-write history is about as unhealthy as it gets.

There are few poems as oft-quoted as Larkin's *This Be The Verse*, not least for the impact of its opening line and the effect parents can have on their child. For me, however, the more damning sentence is the second: 'They may not mean to, but they do.'

Many years ago, I remember talking to a well-known prep school headmaster. Being somewhat new to the nuances of the education world, I put it to him that teaching prep school children represented a unique challenge. 'Oh no', was his instant response. 'You don't realise – educating the children is the easy bit. It's educating the parents, now that's the problem...'

> **Perhaps the hardest part of parenting is knowing when to step back and be confident your child can handle a situation without your help.**

This view might seem harsh but as parents we do need to check ourselves from time to time and ensure we are taking the best path. Of course, being a parent is the hardest challenge any adult will face so we cannot expect to get all the decisions right, all of the time. We need to be kind to ourselves and remember the old adage that a problem shared is a problem halved. And, of course, that's why sharing challenges with school – and working together in partnership so the messaging at home matches that at school – is so important for everyone.

Perhaps the hardest part of parenting is knowing when to step back and be confident your child can handle a situation without your help. Dr Tim Hands, the former Headmaster of Winchester College, summed it up neatly in an article for *Attain*, '...consider your child as a cake: you have provided the very special ingredients, and with great care you have selected the oven which will allow those ingredients to rise to a tasty perfection. Do not now ruin the cake by too frequent an opening of the oven door.' [1]

You know your remarkable child better than anyone. And you know what makes her or him happy. So you are already halfway to finding the right school: their happiness is the key to the whole process.

Attain Guide 2025

Starting the journey

Is your child happy? It may sound a silly question but we should start here as this is the point from which everything else flows. Helen Skrine, the former Headmistress of Belmont Prep in Surrey, summed up happiness in children as follows: 'Healthy and happy children are those who eat and sleep well. They are loved unconditionally, allowed to make mistakes and are learning to be independent in their thoughts and actions. These children are becoming emotionally intelligent and resilient and have the self-knowledge and compassion to form strong relationships. They have high levels of self-esteem and independence, and understand that their self-worth is not bound up in their academic, sporting or artistic achievements but more importantly in meaningful human interactions and their ability to make a contribution and to voice an opinion. Moreover, in the words of the poet Rudyard Kipling, healthy and happy children *...can meet with Triumph and Disaster; And treat those two imposters just the same.*' [2]

It's obvious that happy children succeed and if a child is not happy, he or she will find it much harder to do well at school. So the most important aspect of choosing a school is to find one where your child will be content. All children are different, with wonderful personalities and attributes which combine to make them unique. They like different things and have distinct passions and interests. It's worth reflecting on the times when you see your child at his or her happiest. What are they doing? It's often when undertaking an activity and doing so with other people. It may be sport, art, playing with toys or just running around and being carefree.

One of the foundations of good schools – and particularly those in the independent sector – is the provision of extracurricular activities: those innumerable activities, clubs and teams which are there for children to get involved in while at school. They help fire interests, develop passions and ignite imaginations – and they might end up doing a job in the future linked to one. Yes, academic grades are important but they are often the enabler to being able to pursue a dream. And that dream often starts at school.

In many ways, finding the right school for your child is easy.

There's plenty of choice with amazing institutions offering extraordinary facilities and life-changing opportunities. Like a golden ticket to a future world, they promise so much. Indeed, you might have heard brilliant things about a particular school from friends or neighbours. Or you may have an ambition for your son or daughter to go somewhere you just know in your heart will be right for them. So why does the decision need any further thought?

Quite simply, it feels like one of the biggest decision you will ever make and so you don't want to get it wrong. Some schools have a particular reputation, especially academically, which appeals to some parents. It creates a competitive and pressured market with the idea that winning a place to one of these schools will guarantee a future path of achievement, with a successful career ahead. That isn't always the reality and whilst being ambitious for your child is perfectly natural, it does need to be tempered with ensuring they can cope with the pressure of school – and will be happy.

That point can't be emphasised enough. It's a child's happiness which above all else must lie at the heart of any decision-making. It must temper any hint of parental ambition as only a child who is happy will ultimately succeed. Pushing for a particular senior school will rarely result in happiness if it's not a good match for the child. A small minority of parents can become blinkered in their views and obsess about just one school, especially when it comes to the transition to senior school. One prep school head told me of an occasion when they would not let a parent leave their office until they had specified a second choice senior school, such was the parent's resolute belief their child would win a place at a single, highly coveted, institution. Hours of corrosive tutoring might enable a pupil to get over the admissions hurdle but they will most likely struggle and suffer because of it in the future.

So how do you unpick the process and find the right school? In some ways, it's akin to house-hunting. You can sometimes walk into a house and just get a good feeling about it and know it feels right. Of course, you need to be objective in your thought processes but it's important to trust your instincts, as only you know your child and what makes her or him happy. But you do need to check yourself as even that small minority of parents who are – how shall we put it? – 'overly ambitious' on behalf of their children probably think they are doing it for all the right reasons. Working on the basis that 'they will thank me one day' is not a firm decision-making threshold. Plenty of children gain far better results from not being in a pressured environment, surrounded by others who they feel are better than them – once you feel crushed, it's quite hard to get that self-esteem back.

> **The message is clear – don't overlook those crucial early years and instead appreciate the enormous benefits prep schools can offer to the child.**

The reasons why a parent chooses an independent school are varied. Often, it is the academic breadth and ambitious results; it can also be the range of opportunities available; or it could be that a parent feels it offers their child a supportive setting, especially if they have a particular need, which is just not available elsewhere. Whatever it might be, the fact that private schools are independent – able to follow their own curriculum – gives them significant advantages and flexibility. When looking at school websites, you will see the ubiquitous term 'catering for the needs of the individual' but it's truly something the independent sector can deliver.

Many parents will start their journey at the pre-prep level. Their child will be about five years-old and joining into Reception at either a standalone prep school or one which is part of a larger senior school. Some parents are tempted to skip these early years and switch to the independent sector when their child reaches age 11 or 13. This can be a false economy as many prep schools offer the quality of education in those early and critical years which is difficult to match elsewhere.

But there are also those parents who see prep schools as just a stepping-stone on to the prize of a particularly revered senior school. Indeed, some prep school websites put great emphasis on the destinations of their leavers; far more so than senior schools trumpet their university destinations. Peter Tait, the former Headmaster of Sherborne Prep, was vocal in his criticism of this position, arguing that prep schools are 'the years that count'. He wrote: 'Prep schools should stop labelling themselves as mere feeders and trumpet the fact that prep school is where children learn how to learn, how to think, how to work hard and take responsibility for their own education, so they are better prepared for the straightjacket of public exams that follow.' [3]

The message is clear – don't overlook those crucial early years and instead appreciate the enormous benefits prep schools can offer to the child.

Whatever level you are looking for your child to join – pre-prep, prep or senior – it's perhaps worth remembering one analogy and it involves a swimming pool. You don't want your child to be, metaphorically speaking, in a swimming pool and able to put both feet firmly on the bottom of the pool; it's too comfortable, too relaxed and doesn't require any effort. Equally, you certainly don't want them to end up out of their depth; unable to touch the bottom, unsure what to do and feeling a growing sense of panic. They need the reassurance of knowing their toes can just feel the tiles beneath them if needed. That's when they will grow in confidence and achieve their very best.

Attain Guide 2025

Involving your child

For most parents, they will be approaching the process of choosing a school from the angle of needing to shortlist. But where to begin? You may have heard things from friends about particular schools. Indeed, your child may also have strong views about a future school, especially when it comes to the transition to senior as they may have friends planning on going to a particular school. At a young age, parents are very much having to make a decision in their child's best interests but as they get older, this responsibility shifts; it is therefore unwise not to listen very carefully to your child's views and opinions. The consequences of sending a child to a school they don't wish to attend goes far beyond not succeeding academically. Indeed, your child will often know whether or not it is the right place for her or him by instinct.

We have already established the obvious mantra that happy children succeed so it is counter-productive for parents to pursue an ambition to send a child to a

particular school if the child feels they will be unhappy. The picture becomes more blurred over the question of friends – and wanting to follow in the company of others – especially if it's to a school which parents feel is not the right choice.

Changing school is a huge step and naturally daunting. But life is full of change and it also presents enormous possibilities. For some, it's a chance to throw off the shackles of a previous label and to become the person they aspire to be. Or conversely they may wish to stay with friends and make that change to a new school all together. If the friendship group is healthy and mutually supportive that might be a positive factor; if you fear it's rather more unhelpful, that presents a problem.

One thing is for sure, children are very good at forming friendships from day one at a new school (despite what they may say if this is pointed out to them). Everyone is in the same situation and it's a very important lesson for life. It's also beneficial to have friends outside of school; taking separate paths at senior school doesn't mean the end of a friendship. It can be a very helpful antidote to the pressures of school life to have friends at another school with whom to share reflections during the holidays.

Of course, you know your child better than anyone else and also know what interests him or her. At that all crucial Open Day when they get to tour the school, there will be things they see or hear which will be the tipping point in their decision-making. I am aware of one child who ranks their proposed future senior school on the basis that they allow pupils to eat their pudding before the main course; there are worse reasons for choosing a school but do remember that your child's criteria might not match your own.

Children will also notice things we might not and ask questions we have not even thought about. Some will be linked to particular worries or concerns they have about potentially changing school. There may be things they don't like about their current school and will look to see whether these are the same at a future school. Or they might be looking for reassuring signs that some things are similar between the two schools. Toilets is often a classic, although you would think that as no child seemingly wants to use a mucky toilet, they would collectively look after their school facilities better? Take careful note of their concerns, worries and – hopefully – excitement at some of the possibilities this new school might offer them.

But what of other influences beyond your child? I would like to think that the idea of a parent choosing a school on the basis of a perceived social status has long been relegated to the past. But there is still a hierarchy of – for want of a better word – 'smartness'. It would be easy to draw up a league table (more on those later) of 'smart schools' with all the horrendous clichés that would entail. I can think of a good dozen very smart, traditional preps from where children would only go on to very smart, traditional senior schools. And is that a problem? Not if those are the right choices for those children and they are definitely happy. If it's made for any other reason, it's wrong.

What the neighbours think – or don't think – about your choice of school is irrelevant. When it can become awkward is for families in close-knit communities who choose not to send their child to the local state primary school and opt for independent instead. Watch out for the social backlash that can entail. It takes a brave soul to point out that by not taking up that place at the local primary (to which your child was entitled), you are freeing up resources in the state sector. The argument cuts no sway with those who just see private schools as bastions of privilege, irrespective of whether you are sacrificing everything to pay the fees. There's a lot of politics with school choice.

And whilst parents rate schools in a number of ways, children do the same. Children will order their list based on all sorts of criteria – and not the ones you would think. Some may be unusual but if it matters to him or her it is worth bearing in mind – or providing the reassurance that it's not an issue about which to worry. It can quickly become a complex jigsaw so needs careful discussion; you will need to navigate it with your child, helping them to see all the options whilst listening to their perspectives.

Of course, there might need to be a dose of realism if he or she is thinking of schools which are logistically impossible, financially out of reach or just not a realistic target academically. With the latter, the prep school Head is your friend; his or her advice on whether a possible choice is within grasp is key.

But never overlook your child's amazing eye for spotting the things you might miss. It could just be the deal-breaker or deal-maker.

Elephants in the room

I have yet to meet anyone who doesn't caveat their school days with a negative. It's why all parents want their children to have a better time at school than they did. A few want them to have exactly the same – and at the same institution – which is usually a risky ambition as much will have changed.

Yet despite your school days being such a short period of life, it is without doubt the most transformative. It helps shape you into the adult you will become, often making friends for life along the way. And so it's not surprising that finding the right school for your own child – and being sure of that decision – can feel remarkably difficult.

The good news is that schools today are not like those of thirty-odd years ago. They are genuinely caring and nurturing environments where children are encouraged to do their best and achieve their ambitions. So a lot of the negatives we carry around from our past are unlikely to be experienced by our children.

But they will face new challenges, especially against a backdrop of pervasive social media. Schools today are not perfect and education continues to evolve and develop. For parents however, any parallels with their past schooling will – thankfully – be pretty superficial.

> It's also important to debunk any myths. The worst is the quest for the so-called 'best school'. There is no such thing as the best school for your child, only the right school.

It's also important to debunk any myths. The worst is the quest for the so-called 'best school'. There is no such thing as the best school for your child, only the right school. It might sound a bit trite but you must banish any notions of 'best' and reframe your thinking around finding the right match. And it's a match which works both ways. You cannot mould a child to fit a particular school and if the school is not right for a child, it will only end in unhappiness.

One of the key things to uncover is a school's values. They are not always immediately identifiable and you need to look beyond the marketing to see that they do follow what they purport to do. But nevertheless the values should shine through, particularly when it comes to pastoral care (more on this later). A school should be led by its values and they should permeate throughout all it does. These need to be aligned to your own beliefs – religious or philosophical – and those of your family. After all, these values will be instilled into your child so it's good if you agree with them.

When looking for the right school, you do need to watch out for some unhelpful distractions along the way. You need to be savvy when it comes to school marketing, to see through some of the more slick presentations and keep focused on the facts so you can compare schools directly. It's always important to separate facts from opinions; focus on the former and make your own of the latter. Be careful with any shortcuts – league tables, awards, reviews – you can't outsource the work of making up your mind to someone else. Be cautiously cynical and make sure you are keeping an open mind at all stages.

Another distraction, in my humble opinion, is any discussion of whether co-ed or single sex is the right choice. As a parent, you will have an opinion on this but whether a school is single sex or co-ed is actually secondary to whether it is the right school for your child. Being co-ed or single sex is a key part of its DNA but it doesn't define it and I would suggest that its overall values are not defined by whether it is boys-only, girls-only or both. Don't rule out a school just because it's co-ed or single sex – look at its other benefits first and you might find that it's the right match despite your initial position on this issue.

Of course, for some children, and particularly at certain ages, a single sex setting might work better. For others, co-ed reflects the world outside the school gate and can work equally well for their child. There is no doubt there has been a big shift towards co-education recently, with more schools switching to be fully co-educational or starting with a mixed Sixth Form. Whatever is the case, keep an open mind and don't let this be a factor which influences your shortlist. There are also some schools which have a diamond-model structure whereby the school has a coeducational foundation but boys and girls are taught separately – usually just for the GCSE years – and then brought back together again for the Sixth Form. This can offer some of the advantages that parents seek when choosing a single sex environment but with many of the benefits of coeducation.

> **Don't rule out a school just because it's co-ed or single sex – look at its other benefits first and you might find that it's the right match despite your initial position on this issue.**

The same could be said of boarding. You will know whether your circumstances are such that boarding is a consideration and something you need to factor in. But again it's an ethos and values factor. Boarding schools feel different to day schools – they often serve a much better match tea, that's for sure – as they run 24/7. They tend to have more comprehensive facilities, a greater range of opportunities on offer and a very strong sense of community. But they also tend to be bigger – boarding is expensive to offer unless at scale – and that's reflected in the ethos.

When it comes to deciding on a school, if boarding is a prerequisite, you can simply dismiss day schools. If it might be something for the future, factor it in. All the key issues outlined in this book apply equally whether a school is boarding or day.

> If there is an elephant in the room which gets overlooked, it's whether a school is a good neighbour. And it's one parents would do well to investigate.

If there is an elephant in the room which gets overlooked, it's whether a school is a good neighbour. And it's one parents would do well to investigate. Schools are not sitting in splendid isolation, teaching children behind closed gates and separate from the outside world. They are making future citizens, members of the wider community and when pupils leave, they need to be comfortable in the world outside. So how does a school see itself in the local community?

Do they work with local state schools or offer community service opportunities? There are few more rewarding activities for pupils than spending time in a care home, helping to collect litter, or raising money for charity.

By gaining a sense of service, in the community, they establish a wider sense of self and the ideals and values communities need. I would urge all parents to explore how embedded a school is with the wider community and ask whether it is a good neighbour. It's an elephant which you should not overlook.

And finally, there's one factor left which can spoil the fun of choosing a school. Boring logistics. There's a whole chapter on this later as it's so important. Please don't overlook that commute, the impact of a long car journey everyday and how the school run will impinge on family life. You need to be sure to look at the small things just as much as the large.

If you feel the commute is on the edge of viability, add in the possibility of road works. Small daily frustrations add up to big annoyances – and there is no bigger annoyance than having to withdraw your child as the logistics simply do not add-up. It doesn't matter how good you feel a school might be for your child, if the logistics are unrealistic it shouldn't be on a short list.

But above all else, remember that all-important mantra: *happy children succeed.*

Things to consider

The Head

When it comes to things to consider, the Head is normally pretty high up the list of parental priorities. It boils down to a simple question: do you like her or him? Why this ends-up being a priority in parents' minds is probably down to all those latent issues discussed earlier: the baggage parents unavoidably bring to the process of choosing a school. Bluntly, whether you like the Head or not is actually irrelevant. Far more important is whether they are 'doing a good job' and you have confidence in their leadership of the school.

The situation also shifts slightly depending on the school you are choosing. If you are looking at a small prep school, the Head is someone you will have regular contact with and hear from on a weekly basis at least. If he or she makes your skin crawl that might be a problem. With a large senior school, you may only need to endure contact at a prize-giving or similar event and so it's perfectly possible to get through a five-year stretch and not have much to do with the Head. Where this can be an issue is if you encounter any problems, need to complain and

work with the school – your perception of the Head then comes into sharp relief. One thing is a definite: be wary of choosing a school simply because the major selling point in your mind is how much you like the Head. Great Heads can often stay only five years and they get head-hunted (no pun intended) on to another more 'prestigious' establishment.

Other brilliant Heads do stay for longer – don't be tempted to draw any kind of correlation between longevity in post and performance – but as you will often be making your decision two or more years prior to your child joining, you could have the annoying situation of just settling into school life and finding your dream Head has disappeared into the sunset.

> …you could have the annoying situation of just settling into school life and finding your dream Head has disappeared into the sunset.

So what to do? No doubt your first contact with a Head will be at an Open Day or school visit. Charm exudes and he or she will gush with enthusiasm about their establishment. If they don't, run a mile and cross it off your list. Actually, whilst some Heads can come across as polished sales executives, it's not a part of the job most will relish. Yes, it's always a joy to meet parents (well, usually) but a Head's passion is education and not sales.

They will have mastered the art of diplomacy and small talk is definitely a strong point of headship. They should inspire confidence. You might not like them but you should feel that they have a plan – a programme for running a good school and developing it into the future, plus a clear idea of how your child will fit into that school.

Of course, the small talk does matter. They will be keen to extract from you what you think, your ambitions for your child and – bluntly – whether you are a sensible, well-balanced parent or an overly ambitious nightmare which will cause them considerable time and stress. It's best not to come across as the latter and frame your questions in a sensible way. The Head will be keen to highlight new buildings, achievements and anything shiny to dazzle and delight. It's no bad thing to have thought through in advance what you would like to

Things to consider

ask – how often are the toilets cleaned; do you serve any ultra-processed food; and how robust is your policy on bullying, might be three starters-for-ten? – and if anything is really worrying you about a potential decision, say so.

Heads should be able to provide reassurance and clear up any confusion in your decision-making (one way or the other). And remember: it's often not what's said but what isn't said which provides the most enlightenment.

Having got an impression of the Head, you now need to decide what to do with this information. Keeping in mind he or she might not be at the school forever, it's sensible to have formed an opinion of other key staff who may well be there for the long haul. Deputy Heads can often be someone with whom you would have a lot of contact; they keep the wheels running and a good Head always has brilliant deputies. Really good Deputy Heads often have a habit of going off to be really good Heads – a school from which staff grow and develop in their careers is definitely one to consider strongly.

Class or form teachers are equally important and your child will have more contact with them than the Head. The same is true of house masters and particularly any key boarding staff, if you are not just looking at day schools. Indeed, the actual contact with the Head might be limited to regular newsletters home, small talk at an event or simply a cheery wave across the playground. All in all, this is actually not an issue to sweat about and not having a strong opinion about the Head is equally fine.

> Back in the day, there was one word associated with headship: gravitas. It was a kind of super power – an extra dimension that lesser mortals didn't possess.

That opinion – or lack of it – does of course come from our own school days. What are your memories of your headteachers? Normally the prevailing narrative with early years is someone a bit scary and, when it comes to secondary stage, possibly austere and aloof. Back in the day, there was one word associated with headship: gravitas. It was a kind of super power – an extra dimension that lesser mortals didn't possess. Were they born with it or learnt it at some special school for headteachers: a sort of Hogwarts for Heads?

'Parents want headteachers who are approachable, kind and clearly like children, working with them out of a true vocation,' says Dr Bernard Trafford, the former Headmaster of RGS Newcastle. 'So they want to see someone able to relax with them, to laugh with them, to care and even to cry with them. Nonetheless, the demand for gravitas remains. They want the head to stand on a podium and look the part: to speak out with the authority of an experienced professional against daft government measures, a hostile inspection process, a falsehood in the press; and they want their child's head to back their child and their school to their last breath.' [4]

Unlike our own school days, Heads are much more approachable for children – less strict and severe – and pastoral care is outwardly at the forefront of their role. It's ok to not be ok and the Head genuinely wants to know. That's not to say that they didn't care in the past but the role has shifted as schools have changed.

Was gravitas actually a helpful attribute for headship or just the expectation of leadership? You definitely don't want a cool or trendy Head offering high-fives and being super chilled about everything. But you also don't want someone who appears emotionally dead from the neck up. Something between these two positions is usually best.

> Unlike our own school days, Heads are much more approachable for children – less strict and severe – and pastoral care is outwardly at the forefront of their role.

So, on balance, should you like the Head? If you do, fantastic. Just please don't base your decision on a school entirely on a dreamy view of the Head. If you don't, maybe look at the bigger picture and ask instead if you respect and admire the school and its direction of travel. That's far more important.

And besides, the Head might leave next year.

Things to consider

Pastoral care

The single most important aspect of any school is its pastoral care provision. Whilst many schools will promote their academic excellence as front and centre, it's actually pastoral care – the wellbeing and happiness of pupils – which matters most.

For parents, it is hard to quantitatively assess pastoral care as you cannot see a set of results data, unlike exams, or scan through a list of recent sporting successes, when evaluating extracurricular provision. But what you can do is examine the school's commitment to pastoral care and evaluate how this is embedded – both in the school's ethos and its day-to-day activities.

When you visit a school, if you like the staff you meet, are impressed by the pupils and their attitude and character, and feel that it's a supportive and inclusive community, you are witnessing first-hand the results of its pastoral care provision. Pastoral care really consists of two aspects, which are intertwined and mutually

dependent. The first is a nurturing and caring environment which extends a network of help and support around all members of the school community. The second is the instilling of values which helps the pupils to develop in character and feeds back into the supportive environment for all. These two strands of pastoral care are both equally important and rely on each other to thrive.

> Parents should look in detail at how pastoral care is offered in a school and ask appropriate questions. If my child is unhappy, how will they be supported?

Good schools therefore have a very integrated approach to pastoral care, embedding themes and concepts throughout the timetable, often in subtle and creative ways.

Let's look at the welfare provision in schools first. At all good schools, whether prep or senior, there will be key staff responsible for day-to-day wellbeing and to whom pupils can turn if they have problems. Many prep schools will have a School Counsellor who provides more in-depth pastoral support, guiding and helping pupils navigate challenges in their life whilst at school. At senior schools, there is an expanded support network, all working together to provide a range of assistance and interventions tailored to the needs of an individual pupil.

Parents should look in detail at how pastoral care is offered in a school and ask appropriate questions. If my child is unhappy, how will they be supported? Who do parents talk to when their child encounters challenges and needs help from school? With pastoral care at prep level, it's most effective when offered in partnership with parents, especially when navigating issues around friendship and emotional development. It's so important that values and messaging are hand-in-hand so there is continuity between school and home. Working with school ensures this consistency and helps children navigate some of the issues of growing up and becoming more independent.

This supportive environment is paramount and many good schools ensure that as well as strong links between families and school there are also strong top-down links, with older pupils supporting younger ones, often through careful role modelling to ensure pupils help and support each other.

One area which can clearly show a school's commitment to pastoral care is how it deals with any issues of bullying. Sadly, it always exists in one form or another and the important thing is to discover not whether it exists in a school (it will) but how situations are dealt with, pupils educated, and the values and behaviours which are inculcated to help prevent occurrences in the future. Whilst you can get some sense of pastoral care by looking at a school's website, you will get a much better feel for these values when you visit, normally at an Open Day. In the same way that you can get an understanding of whether a school will be a good fit for your child, you can get a sense of whether its pastoral care provision chimes with your values.

If you are looking at boarding, pastoral care extends beyond the confines of the normal day and will have specific systems in place for weekend activities. There should always be someone for your child to talk to if they have a problem and who will be looking out for them and checking they are happy. An Open Day is the chance to meet some of these people and for both you and your child to see if you like them and whether the school would be a good fit for their needs.

> **…pastoral care has a second strand beyond the supportive and caring environment and that is the teaching of values, which feeds back into life at the school.**

As outlined at the beginning, pastoral care has a second strand beyond the supportive and caring environment and that is the teaching of values, which feeds back into life at the school. These values are taught alongside the promotion of health and wellbeing, both physical and mental. Together, this helps pupils face challenges both at school and beyond by growing in resilience. Another aspect is exploring pupils' role in the community and wider world; the importance of community service, helping others and being a good friend and future citizen.

Pupils need to understand the importance of equality, diversity and inclusion; and they need to celebrate and respect difference. These qualities, combined with an understanding of life beyond the school gate, help foster values of tolerance, empathy and understanding, all of which are crucial to being good future citizens.

> **Sport can play a key role in the physical wellbeing of pupils, regardless of whether a child sees themselves as 'sporty' or not. Parents should find out the range of activities on offer and will quickly get a sense of whether it will suit their child.**

Sport can play a key role in the physical wellbeing of pupils, regardless of whether a child sees themselves as 'sporty' or not. Parents should find out the range of activities on offer and will quickly get a sense of whether it will suit their child. For some schools, sport is a very strong and important part of their DNA; others play hard but offer a more inclusive mix of options. You will know – and your child will certainly tell you – where their sporting ambitions lie. For wellbeing, regular exercise and PE is designed to encourage fitness, confidence and help boost mental health.

Put together, these two strands of pastoral care combine to create a wonderful environment of respect and nurture which ensures pupils really thrive during their time at school. You can only evaluate it in person, by talking to staff and pupils and truly getting a sense of what's on offer.

When pastoral care is done well, it creates the right environment for happy children to succeed.

Things to consider

Curriculum

If there is one aspect which is often overlooked when choosing schools – or just taken for granted – it's a school's curriculum. Parents might assume that the curriculum at all independent schools is the same – why would it be different? In fact, curricula is one of the areas which most defines the individuality of independent schools and gives them distinctiveness and identity. You can tell a lot about a school by precisely what it teaches – and what it does not.

Let's start with prep schools. The whole purpose of a prep school curriculum is to foster a love of learning. It covers all the basics of the National Curriculum but, by being independent, it has the freedom to go further and look beyond the basic topics. Good prep schools develop intellectual curiosity in pupils and this is helped by having subject specialist teachers. During these formative years, children begin to learn the skills of independent study and enquiry. They learn to disseminate information quickly, decode problems and put forward logical and well-developed arguments. And they also start to develop the discipline of using time properly and efficiently. They learn how to learn.

As well as these fundamentals, good prep schools also have plenty of space beyond the core subjects of English, maths and science. Many will offer multiple languages, keen to develop the linguistic capabilities of pupils. Others will also offer traditional subjects such as classics, which provide skills beneficial to other disciplines.

> **Look carefully at any prep school curriculum and ensure that it pays equal measure to the creative as well as the academic.**

Prep schools have particularly strong resources in creative subjects such as art, design and technology, and music. These subjects are not soft options but help to develop skills in creative thinking and problem solving. Look carefully at any prep school curriculum and ensure that it pays equal measure to the creative as well as the academic. If a subject is dropped at some point, do ask why and be sure you feel comfortable with this.

Underpinning all these subjects will be effective ICT provision, giving pupils strong digital skills in the tools they need to be effective communicators. They will develop the ability to research, present work and learn programming skills. They will normally have access to laptops and tablets. Ask about a school's approach to digital learning, how this extends to the home environment and where parents can support.

Of course, at the heart of any good curriculum are the teachers who deliver it. Independent schools have traditionally been able to recruit exceptional teachers, with a passion for their subject and who go above and beyond to deliver it. That might not universally be the case and only you can tell at an Open Day whether the teachers you meet are inspiring and would help instil a sense of passion in a particular topic. It's no bad idea to ask a pupil tour guide who is their favourite teacher – and why.

We have already touched upon the temptation for parents to miss out the prep school years, when faced with the huge cost of independent education. Prep school heads will tell you that this is actually a false economy but this message is sometimes not reinforced enough. As Peter Tait, former Headmaster of Sherborne Prep, wrote in *Attain*: 'This is attributable in part to the widespread mythology that spending on education becomes more important the older children get. Senior schools seldom acknowledge how much of their success is due to the prep school children who have been sent to them. It is also due to the erroneous belief that education should work from the top down rather than from the bottom up... And in part, it is due to prep schools not getting the message out that they are not mere 'feeders', preparing children for a more important place, but that they are that important place.'[5]

Traditionally, prep schools prepared pupils for entrance to senior school through the Common Entrance examination. This was the rite of passage exit examination at 13+. Today, there is a much broader range of examination options with 11+ entry to senior school and many preps adopting skills-based and values-based curricula, such as the Pre-Senior Baccalaureate (PSB).

Frameworks like the PSB encourage independent learning, critical thinking, communication, collaboration and leadership, all centred around a skills grid. The curriculum a prep school follows is very much part of its core values and you need to think about whether the overall approach to learning is one which resonates with you, knowing your child's aptitudes.

> **A key part of the prep school years is the preparation for senior school but, to make this the focus, is to lose the value of the journey along the way.**

One final caveat is to watch out for any indication that a school has a narrowness of purpose or unhealthy focus on the pursuit of academic goals. A key part of the prep school years is the preparation for senior school but to make this the focus, is to lose the value of the journey along the way. And this journey is a really long one – anything up to nine years if a child starts at Reception and goes through to age 13.

In your choice of prep, you do therefore want to make sure that any temptation for narrow specialisation is avoided as this will not help pupils in the long run. And do remember that balance between the traditional academic subjects and the creative arts; they should sit side by side, enhancing each other.

The same argument is true when it comes to assessing the curriculum at senior school. Unlike the early years, where there is much more freedom, the focus will be on GCSEs. That doesn't necessarily mean a narrowing of focus and look for how creativity is maintained and the range of GCSE choices on offer. As a child progresses through school, there is a narrowing – or funnel effect – as subject choices dictate the need to specialise. But whatever a child's talents, ensuring as broad a range of subject choices as possible keeps equally as many doors open for the future. Careers are changing but you won't hear employers lamenting a candidate's broad knowledge or wide subject breadth.

> **But whatever a child's talents, ensuring as broad a range of subject choices as possible keeps equally as many doors open for the future.**

Of course, your child's interests at 11 or 13 will undoubtedly change but pay careful note to see which subjects can be continued through to GCSE. A clear passion for the social sciences would be undermined if these cannot be pursued fully. Equally, can art and DT be followed through to GCSE or do you need to choose one or the other? Together this gives you a good indication of focus by the school and where its academic priorities lie.

A similar situation is true at A Level but many senior schools offer a huge range of A Level or IB options. They will have considerable experience in preparing pupils for university entrance not just in the UK but overseas. Does this school feel like it might cater for your child's interests, regardless of the direction they might follow? And what about for those pupils who don't seek a university place and want to either enter straight into employment, start a business or pursue a different route entirely? Are their interests and ambitions championed and celebrated as much as those who seek the dreaming spires?

Examination results obviously matter, but too strong a focus on grades runs the risk of failing to develop imaginative, curious thinkers. In a fast changing world, what skills do employers value most?

Extracurricular

There is nothing 'extra' about 'extracurricular'. It's not the icing on the cake but more the sugar and jam filling – without it, the cake would be bland and a bit tasteless. When it comes to extracurricular provision, it is definitely more than the sum of its parts. On first glance, it can look a bit like a list of hobbies or fun after school activities. But the benefits pupils gain can have hugely positive rewards, sometimes opening their eyes to the possibilities for a future career.

One of the biggest extracurricular activities at most schools is sport. Schools will have a clear programme of sports, centred around the seasons, and with competitive team games. With some school sports, representation goes to the highest level with county or national selection. The majority of children will not play these sports again when they leave school but the values of camaraderie, teamwork and fair play will have (hopefully) had a positive impact for life.

Good schools offer a programme of sport for all – not just a subset of those who have a greater aptitude. When you visit a school, ask which sports are compulsory and what your child will likely be playing – at what stages do they have choice and can pursue individual interests?

> **When you visit a school, ask which sports are compulsory and what your child will likely be playing – at what stages do they have choice and can pursue individual interests?**

The prep school years are very important here as it can be a time when children start to develop a keen interest in sport but, managed badly, children can also turn against it and see sport as a negative. It should be a happy experience for everyone, regardless of their sporting ability, and the key is to make it inclusive for all.

Whilst sport often takes the limelight, music and drama are usually very strong at most independent schools. The opportunities for individual music tuition, in multiple instruments, as well as orchestras, ensembles and other bands, gives pupils the chance to develop a passion and outlet for expression in music. It shouldn't just be about the pursuit of grades however and the mindful and relaxing benefits of music are hugely important. After a busy day, the opportunity to unwind by becoming absorbed in playing an instrument for pleasure – and not as a chore or after constant nagging from parents – is a wonderful outlet for self-expression and relaxation.

Among all the prep schools nationally are over 20 choir schools, with a national reputation for musical excellence, developing the vocal skills of pupils and providing a rich and historic setting for choral music. Being a chorister can be a wonderful opportunity and well worth exploring for families; the flip side is that whilst it usually comes with considerable fee remission, it requires a huge family commitment with much free time put into choir practice and services.

Drama is always strong in independent schools, with some offering extraordinary facilities to pupils for dramatic art, extremely professional productions and highly specialist teachers. Opportunities exist both on stage and behind the scenes and it can spark a passion for the arts which continues well into adulthood. In addition to drama, LAMDA offers pupils the chance to build confidence and perform to a crowd. Learning how to communicate to an audience with a relaxed and clear delivery, especially if learnt early, is of incredible benefit to helping to overcome anxiety and boost confidence. Strong presentation skills are highly sought-after by employers and, through activities like LAMDA, poetry recitals and debating, pupils can leave with this added to their skillset.

Sport, music and drama are the major extracurricular areas but what about the myriad other activities which enrich pupils lives? Compare and contrast on school websites and you find everything and anything from creative writing to chess, fencing to yoga, cooking to film clubs, ceramics to Combined Cadet Force, Duke of Edinburgh's Award to sailing. The lists are endless and very, very impressive.

Good schools encourage children to try any activity they think they might enjoy; there is no harm in not liking it and switching to something else. Some may come with a cost, all of which ends up on the end of term bill. But with that cost comes an interest, a passion and possibly the creative spark for the future. As adults, the hurdles of time and money to be able to try just one of these activities again puts most out of reach. The extracurricular provision is one of those areas where it's easy to say that children don't realise just how lucky they are to have all these amazing options available.

> **The extracurricular provision is one of those areas where it's easy to say that children don't realise just how lucky they are to have all these amazing options available.**

One extracurricular activity which is obviously not highlighted but worth remembering is boredom. Don't be tempted – or allow your child – to cram too much into the day. Yes, there are all these options available and it's brilliant to be able to pursue them but, at the same time, downtime and relaxation is vital. And we don't hear enough about the importance of boredom – or more precisely, unstructured downtime and relaxation – the opportunity to make your own fun, to sit and read, or do nothing of significance except to reflect on the day and process everything which has happened. The extracurricular is about exploring interests and building passions; it isn't about putting together a CV.

> **The extracurricular is about exploring interests and building passions; it isn't about putting together a CV.**

Another aspect of the extracurricular is the chance to visit other places linked to a subject topic, as well as residential trips. Residentials, especially when undertaken in the prep years, help to build confidence and independence.

It's a big deal being away from home the first time and they are great for gradually introducing this and making it an enjoyable and transformative experience. So whilst it might be just a trip for a few nights to a particular destination, the personal and social skills this offers are far greater than the face-value

experience. Trips and activities like this often require working collectively with others and help promote qualities such as leadership and self-discovery.

Pupils can learn much about compassion and the need to think of others less fortunate through extracurricular activities linked to community service and charity. In the senior years, this might involve a visit to a care home, or helping fundraise with a charity, enabling pupils to see directly how they can support others.

And so when you put all these qualities and values together – which lie at the heart of any extracurricular programme – you very quickly realise why they offer far more than the sum of their parts.

Things to avoid

Marketing spin

Look at many independent school websites and you will find a deluge of photographs of happy, smiling children. You will be taken on a journey of slick marketing showing you insights into the school, highlights of pupil success and ambition. You will almost certainly have to grapple with a navigation which is more style over substance, a lavish design not unlike a luxury consumer brand, logos for awards which sound good but you don't actually know the value, and possibly a presentational video which feels more like an episode of *Made in Chelsea* than a serious attempt to convey what it means for your son or daughter to study at the school. Welcome to the world of school marketing.

Actually, to be fair, it's often worse than this. I have looked through hundreds of school websites and it often takes several minutes to actually find the age at which they start admitting pupils. In an ever increasing spiral of marketing gloss, the key messages risk being forgotten. For the prospective parent, you need clear and concise information so you can make an

informed decision. Instead, you often have to wade through pages of slick media before you begin to get a proper insight. Too many schools are not even thinking of the reality of the time-pressured, somewhat stressed parent whose appetite for browsing is limited – not through choice but necessity. Some websites might look nice but they feel bloated, too slick and lack authenticity.

> **Some websites might look nice but they feel bloated, too slick and lack authenticity.**

So what do you need to actually find on a school website? Admissions is the key section. It should set out the 'who, why, what, where and when' of the process, ideally with a helpful timeline, so you can assess what is involved. There is usually a registration cost, deadlines, fees breakdown by year group and an indication of what is considered extras on the bill. You can then clearly see what's involved and the financial implications. The next thing to look at is ethos. But how do you try and ascertain the ethos and values of a school from its website?

I would suggest starting with the Head's message. It introduces you to her or him and lets you start to develop a picture of the school. They can often be quite formulaic but some are more quirky and interesting. A good welcome message will tell you something of the personality of the Head as well as the personality of the school – where is the emphasis placed and does this sit comfortably with what you know are your child's aptitudes?

The next thing to find is the extracurricular provision. As discussed in the last chapter, this is a key aspect of any school and gives you a huge insight into priorities and the level of provision available to pupils. You should be able to delve into detail about sport, music, drama and other activities. Browse and get a sense of what is available and when your child would be able to do some of these things. How much is embedded as part of the curriculum and how many are choices reserved for after school clubs?

You might also come across some useful notices to give you an insight into transport links and any school bus provision, pastoral care structure, the food menu, environmental initiatives or community service. Together these all provide valuable background into life at the school.

Before you leave the school website – and assuming you have been impressed so far – it's time to look at the more boring but very important information from which to begin any due diligence. You need to find the Inspections section and look at the latest inspection report, which highlights the academic and pastoral performance of the school. These can appear quite daunting and we unpack the details in a later chapter, but it's a crucial document with which to make assessments. Alongside the inspections, you will often find other key policy documents which provide useful reading.

For financial reporting, you need either to be looking at Companies House or the Charity Commission website if the school is a registered charity. Why bother? You are going to be spending a sum of money, over many years, which will (most likely) be the single biggest investment you make, apart from your home. So you cannot ignore the financial health of the organisation and should consult all the publicly available records. We look at how to find these in more detail, alongside inspection reports, in a later chapter.

So you now have a sense of the ethos, values, academic and pastoral performance, financial integrity and the extent of extra-curricular opportunities. You might also have been treated to endless drone footage of sports pitches. Is there anything else to look at whilst online? You can certainly consult the school's social media channels – take your pick as few leave any base uncovered – and your sleuthing will reward you with some potentially interesting news snippets. Does the social media output match with what you have discovered through your research and are they communicating to you? Does it give you genuine insight into the life of the school and does it feel authentic and real?

> **The challenge for prospective parents is to cut through the marketing and reach your target: does this honestly feel like a potentially suitable school for my child?**

The challenge for prospective parents is to cut through the marketing and reach your target: does this honestly feel like a potentially suitable school for my child? Having made your own assessment, why not then let your child have the opportunity to explore the site and get his or her own sense of what's on offer. Ask them to make a few notes and then see what they have discovered and highlighted. Of course, they are unlikely to head straight to the inspection report or start trawling the Charity Commission data but they might just surprise you with what they discover. In just the same way that they have a special insight when it comes to in-person visits, they may spot something online which proves very interesting. You need to keep your more cynical and discerning approach but it is also worth seeing how any marketing spin works on your child. Do they buy into it or do they manage to look beyond the branding and spot what is valuable to them?

> **There is one very important offline activity you should do for any school you think might be worth considering: get hold of a copy of the school magazine.**

There is one very important offline activity you should do for any school you think might be worth considering: get hold of a copy of the school magazine. It might be available online but if not, contact the Admissions team and ask if you can be sent a printed copy or call in and collect one if local. It's a wonderful source of information as it will often contain articles written by pupils, details of school trips, expeditions and activities undertaken by different year groups. You will get a sense of the community, the spirit and, crucially, the values.

A good school magazine gives you everything you need to assess what it stands for and believes in. As it is aimed at current parents and pupils it tends (although sadly not always) to be less slick and polished from a marketing perspective. Whilst it's never going to be a 'warts and all' account, you can read between the lines. It will showcase the best examples of pupil work and all the achievements the school is proud to celebrate.

Compare one school magazine with another and you can start to make assessments of the things which have been happening (or not happening) and if these are valuable to you and your child. Crucially, does a school feel like a happy and inclusive community, celebrating individual success and achievement? That's for you to decide.

Things to avoid

League tables

What if there was a way to bypass this long tortuous process of choosing a school? What if someone very kindly compiled a list of all the schools in an area and put them in order of academic performance? After all, academic performance is purportedly the thing parents are most interested in – it's the pathway to university and beyond. It spells success for life, doesn't it? Parents could quickly cast their eye down this magical list and see what's on offer and instantly decide to go for the one at the very top. After all, why hang around the third division when you could be pushing for the premier league, eh?

And so that's what happened. And this idea grew and grew to become a regular annual occurrence across several newspapers – even the Government got in on the idea on the basis of that Whitehall favourite: accountability. And despite the opposition to this annual bonanza of ranking and sorting, it continues unabated. It even purports to tell you which schools are 'on the rise' and those who have, sadly, 'slipped' any number of places. But what's the problem with this, I hear you ask? It works well for football teams, what about schools? After all, reading the newspaper articles which accompany the ranking tables, you could be left with the impression they are providing parents with empirical data from which to make informed and enlightened decisions. Does it not hold the feet to the fire for schools who so loudly claim academic excellence? Does it not show clearly the return on investment for parents?

Er, no. It shows none of these things. It's a whole load of empirical nonsense which provides short term boasting for some but only for as long as nobody challenges what exactly they are congratulating themselves about or pokes holes in the implied arguments. League tables look as if they are telling you lots of important information and enabling you to make direct comparisons in your search for the best school. Indeed, you would be forgiven for thinking they actually highlight the very best schools in the country. But like most things, you need to look behind and understand what's missing. You then quickly realise they are a false friend.

> **It's a whole load of empirical nonsense which provides short term boasting for some but only for as long as nobody challenges what exactly they are congratulating themselves about or pokes holes in the implied arguments.**

Dr Tim Hands, former Headmaster of Winchester College (and previously Master of Magdalen College School) wrote the following for *Attain*: 'The principal problem with league tables is that they appear to tell you, with all the clarity of the sports pages, which outfit or team is performing best. In fact, they tell you very little about that team at all. They tell you about output – as measured by public exam results, which are themselves imperfect indicators – but they tell you nothing about academic input. And they measure only one part of a school's output: they tell you nothing about pastoral care, extracurricular activity, facilities, finances, career progression, tone, or anything else.' [6]

And that's the problem. Academic output – the grades achieved by pupils in public examinations – sounds like a useful benchmark. Except that it falls over by what is included and, crucially, excluded. Take these scenarios: what about schools who enter pupils for exams, such as modern languages or maths, a year early? Are these results carried through or separately highlighted? What about schools who challenge some pupils' results (which lots of independent schools do) and are awaiting these potential re-grades? What about schools who do not take A Levels and opt for the IB instead – can you compare the two? What about the IGCSE and any other examinations which might be excluded and cannot be compared? And what about schools who opt out of sharing their data, for whatever reason? The league tables don't give you the full picture.

Some schools see their academic success as their *raison d'être* – take away league tables and they might easily feel you cut off their best marketing tool for prospective parents. But would you really do this? The argument only works if parents continue to be fed league tables with the implied premise that it equips them to make decisions about their child's future schooling. It does not.

There have been calls for reform for years and years. Some have suggested that only a five-year average for each school should be published as it would giver greater insight. But the reality of this longer period of comparison is that it would simply highlight the level of academic selection on entry to the top performing schools. What would it tell you about schools lower down the perceived hierarchy who might be achieving wonderful things with a less selective intake? Nothing. And more over, what would it tell you about your own child, if she or he were to go to a particular school? Zero.

> **What's the point of spending a moment looking at these things if it tells you absolutely nothing of benefit in your search for a school for your individual child.**

And surely that's the rub. What's the point of spending a moment looking at these things if it tells you absolutely nothing of benefit in your search for a school for your individual child. It doesn't help you to evaluate their needs and whether those listed are best placed to support them. But it fills newspapers and creates news stories, so that's nice.

> Some Heads feel it would be better not to have league tables at all. Schools could instead simply publish their own set of results, alongside a national average or median score: no ranking in tables, no pointless comparisons.

Some Heads feel it would be better not to have league tables at all. One solution is that schools could instead simply publish their own set of results, alongside a national average or median score: no ranking in tables, no pointless comparisons. The bandwagon would finally stop. Crucially, it would still provide total transparency which parents absolutely have the right to seek. But what they don't need is unhelpful comparisons, dressed up as enlightened insight.

Parents reasonably assume that league tables are worthwhile and provide the transparency they need when choosing a school. The sad fact is that the bandwagon keeps going because of the power of marketing. Some schools think they need league tables because the governors think it provides useful marketing and so the demand creates the supply. In fact, the thing that parents should look at is a school's university entrance success to effectively judge its academic performance. They also must attach as much weight to looking at a school's success in sport, music, drama and all manner of other extracurricular activities. But do be mindful that we are at a turning point when university entrance is no longer the be-all and end-all for progressing on to all manner of careers and vocations. Success comes in many forms.

I will leave the last word to Tim Hands: 'League tables look helpful to any prospective parent. But parents, heed this unequivocal word of warning, from one whose school has often been at the top of such tables: don't invest a shred of trust in tables.' [6]

Things to avoid

Unhelpful influences

Awards are great. And winning awards is even better. The pride and acknowledgment to be chosen as the best deserves recognition and praise. In independent education you have dedicated and committed staff going above and beyond to create the very best educational opportunities for children. Schools are often innovative and creative places, pioneering new ideas for teaching, curriculum and pastoral care. All these things matter and deserve to be championed and celebrated.

The problem comes with how awards are used in marketing. Prospective parents will often see awards on school websites, highlighting winners or shortlisted schools. But winners of what exactly, how many entered and what specifically were the criteria? Glibly claiming to be 'the best' when not all peers entered an award gives the wrong impression. Awards are big commercial undertakings and there's money to be made. And it's because of this that it can shift from being a

worthy and enlightened process to one of commercial objectives, with entry fees, awards dinners and sponsorship opportunities. Arguably, the award organisers gain the most from the whole awards bandwagon.

From the parental perspective, what does it all mean when faced with a slogan which tells you that a particular school was shortlisted for 'best private school 2024'? Does this mean that this school is the best school in the country? Does this mean that this school has been judged in all areas against all the other independent schools of its type? And even more bluntly, does this mean that it's the right school for your child? In posing these questions, that's not to say that the recipient isn't an excellent school, worthy of praise at the very highest level. But for the prospective parent it means little to actually help them in deciding if a school is a good fit for their individual child. It may be worth considering alongside all the other schools which fit your criteria but, in and of itself, this slogan helps little.

It gets worse when it gets more granular. There are now awards for seemingly everything and anything. Yet not actually for things which would be helpful for a prospective parent. Still no sign of an award for the 'school with the smallest percentage fee increase over the last decade'. Being declared 'best school in the south west for the creative arts' means what exactly? It presupposes that all the other schools from Somerset to Land's End have taken part and, when the scores were in, this one came out on top. And we are talking creative arts here, not maths, so it's entirely subjective.

> There are now awards for seemingly everything and anything. Yet not actually for things which would be helpful... Still no sign of an award for the 'school with the smallest percentage fee increase over the last decade'

Some awards are linked to league tables, which is doubly unhelpful for prospective parents as league tables simply measure educational output. They don't tell you about input nor, frankly, whether a school is the right one for your child's needs. At best, these sorts of granular awards highlight where a school might have a particular strength but, of course, overlook those who haven't entered.

And the same problem exists with reviews, another area which has grown exponentially in recent years. Previously, you might find one or two reviews of a school, written for a particular publication. You knew the target readership and so could read and interpret accordingly, knowing it might add a little 'additional flavour' to your perspective. But not now. Reviews today are another big business and prospective parents need to raise more than just an eyebrow when looking at some of these.

> Some restaurant reviews are absolute howlers but curiously I have yet to read a poor – or frankly critical – review of an independent school.

Just ask yourself the obvious questions: who wrote this and in what way were they qualified to review a school? I have worked for the independent education sector for twenty-five years and I wouldn't dream of writing a review of a school. But I do know how to find the right one for your child and (spoiler alert) it doesn't involve reviews. Perhaps the most important point, which hangs over any collection of reviews: what is the commercial motivation behind this venture and how does it help schools?

Now that isn't to say that some reviews have no merit at all. Reading a review can sometimes be enlightening and provide additional facts which a parent might not have gleaned from the school website. But it's not like a restaurant review in a Sunday paper. Food, unlike education, is a much more tangible and straightforward thing to review. Yes, people have differing tastes but it's pretty easy to work through this and discern from a review if a restaurant is the sort of place you might like to visit.

Some restaurant reviews are absolute howlers but curiously I have yet to read a poor – or frankly critical – review of an independent school. The common theme is a gushing, thesaurus-infused opinion piece which seems solely to provide a marketing pat on the back. And that's absolutely fine if you like that sort of thing and read it in that context. But if you are wanting to read a rigorous independent review of a school, you need to look at its inspection report instead.

Inspection reports might seem a bit dull and impenetrable. They don't have the pithy soundbites, elated praise or joyous overtones of many school reviews. Whilst inspections can never be perfect they do provide the conclusions of a rigorous and robust process which took place over several days and was conducted by a group of trained education inspectors. Their judgment, against a published inspection framework, provides a basis for comparison and understanding. The reports are not gushing and effusive but that isn't their purpose. We will discuss how to read an inspection report in a later chapter.

> Alongside the awards and reviews, there is another corrosive element which has grown significantly recently: the rise of the brand.

Alongside the awards and reviews, there is another corrosive element which has grown significantly recently: the rise of the brand. School branding has gone from the justifiable need for clarity of image identity and consistent communications to the adoption of branding approaches normally reserved to luxury labels. It can often feel overly slick and pushy. Too much style over substance comes at the cost of authenticity.

Looking at all of this from the school's perspective, they are often caught in a bind. It's a commercial world and if one of their rival schools is making noise on social media about being shortlisted for 'cleanest minibus in the south east', they will feel they need to follow suit for fear that prospective parents might conclude their minibus is far from spotless. If you win an award, you might as well highlight it. It seems silly to stick it on the shelf and not tell people, regardless of what you might privately feel about it. If all your rival schools have multiple reviews, you will worry that you don't have the same. And if a rival school launches a new brand identity which makes them look super stylish with ultra-slick imagery, shouldn't you do similar? Will parents judge a school by its branding or will they step back and think objectively?

Of course, it's like judging a book by its cover but we live in a world of marketing noise. I do wish some schools would give parents the chance to make their decisions without the unhelpful influence of marketing spin and ditch the need for any hype.

Things to avoid

Parental pressure

In the first chapter of this book, I referenced Larkin's *This Be The Verse* as it's something which often comes into my mind as a parent. It's not the first expletive-laden line which has the impact but the second sentence: 'They may not mean to, but they do.' And at the heart of that is often the problem of parental pressure.

You love and cherish your child. You want the very best for him or her and you want them not to fail or be upset; to achieve in areas where perhaps you didn't. You encourage them and nurture them; try and give them all the opportunities to find their passions and interests so they can succeed and be happy. But in the vortex of school life, that encouragement can become unhealthy and too pressured if you don't regularly check yourself. You can always see it in others – the parent who encourages too much, that unhealthy vicarious ambition writ large. But how do you see it in yourself? How do you get the balance right between encouragement and being too

pushy? And the area where this becomes the most problematic is when it comes to the transition from prep to senior school.

Undoubtedly the issue is external pressure. There is always competition for places at excellent schools which drives up demand, worry and anxiety. Parents make a judgment about which school they would like their child to aim towards and it might be a stretch. There is an assessment hurdle to overcome: can they do it? Are they falling behind in a key subject – maybe maths is the weakness, or verbal reasoning needs more encouragement. Is their current school appearing to support them enough? Maybe we should get a tutor?

And so it begins. Six simple words – *maybe we should get a tutor?* – but the impact of that rhetorical question can be immense. It should actually be: maybe we should talk to school? When everyone else is doing extra maths, weekend and evening tutoring, it's a very brave and confident parent who doesn't seek the assessment of a tutor. And the tutor will indeed find gaps in the child's learning. But find a child who doesn't have gaps. And that's why you need to think twice and whatever you do must be in partnership with the current school including, most definitely, any judgement regarding which senior schools might be the most sensible options. As parents, you can be too close to be objective whereas school is best placed to step back and make realistic judgments. That isn't to say that school will be lacking in ambition for your child. Far from it. But they will also know when too much might indeed be too much.

> **As parents, you can be too close to be objective whereas school is best placed to step back and make realistic judgments. That isn't to say that school will be lacking in ambition for your child. Far from it. But they will also know when too much might indeed be too much.**

Getting into a coveted senior school isn't about clearing a hurdle and the hard work is done. That's just the beginning. If a child cannot maintain that standard and progress further on the same trajectory, they will feel a constant, unrealistic pressure to succeed. And what will be the impact if they perceive that all those around them are always achieving more? It is far better to be in a school where a child feels comfortable with the pace of learning than to be grappling to achieve, surrounded by others who seem not to struggle.

The first – and hardest – thing is to ascertain if your aspirations for your child are right. You should set this high and want your child to fly. But set them too high and they will suffer as a result, even if your child manages to overcome the hurdle of entrance exams. In almost every chapter of this book, the importance of happiness is repeated and for good reason. Being unhappy through pressure, feeling that you are not at the same level as peers or just not successful is crushing and hugely detrimental to a child's welfare.

Many children will succeed by all number of benchmarks in the long run but, through differences in learning, reach these milestones through a different route or slightly later. It doesn't make it wrong or not as good as other approaches. Be open-minded and find the learning environment with which your child will feel comfortable. And always work hand-in-hand with your child's current school.

Peter Tait, former Headmaster of Sherborne Prep wrote: 'Common sense and parental instinct have always been the best guides to raising children. But parents also need to have confidence in those whose job it is to look after their children's education. To do this requires a certain detachment, a willingness to trust the passage of time, focusing on whether their children are happy, challenged and purposeful and are learning the right values. If so, they will be fine.' [7]

> And patience is very much a virtue. Children cannot be rushed and, for some, learning may take a little longer to reach the same level as others.

And patience is very much a virtue. Children cannot be rushed and, for some, learning may take a little longer to reach the same level as others. 'Above all, parents need to be patient; they need to temper their aspirations for their children and not put undue pressure on them,' says Peter Tait. 'There is a temptation to think that if children work harder, get more help, be put under a bit more pressure, they can improve their marks and get into the school the parents wanted. The dangers of doing so, however, are manifest and can severely damage a child's well-being.' [8]

Finally, it is worth remembering that when it comes to tutoring, senior schools are very wise to the pressures put on children. They can tell if a pupil has been over-prepared and isn't being their authentic self; they are trained to sniff out over-tutoring a mile off.

guidance and support. There may be circumstances when tutoring might be beneficial for a particular pupil's situation. But if so, it should be done with the full support of the school and the individual subject teachers. Done this way, everyone is on the same page: pupil, parent, tutor and the school.

The relationship with school is a partnership and they will help you nurture your child to become a genuine, confident, happy and curious pupil with a desire to learn. And isn't that exactly what senior schools are looking for when it comes to an interview?

> ...when it comes to tutoring, senior schools are very wise to the pressures put on children. They can tell if a pupil has been over-prepared and isn't being their authentic self; they are trained to sniff out over-tutoring a mile off.

So whatever the temptation, it is worth pausing and working closely with the prep school instead. Seek their advice,

Practical aspects

Logistics

With your research done and shortlist coming along nicely, it might be an opportunity to relax. Except that there is one more factor to consider and it might appear a bit dull. It's easy to dismiss 'logistics' as unimportant and not one of the big questions to answer. It can feel like a distraction which might spoil the fun. Well, it's not fun being a party pooper but this chapter is all about the world of logistics. Or getting from A to B and, should that journey get to be too much, whether boarding might be a suitable solution. And the reason that logistics matters is that it can help ensure that everything flows: the prep gets done on time and your child awakes after a good night's sleep ready for the next school day.

Much depends on where you live. School needs to be within easy reach and the precise method of journey can often shift as a child gets older. In the younger prep

school years, it will probably involve the car and then there may be a school bus option for later. But that car journey is important to consider. How long will it take and how much time will be spent sitting in traffic? For a child, this time adds up and becomes very tiring. It's no surprise that few Reception age children can remember what they had for lunch on a given day – so much has been happening and they are genuinely exhausted by 3pm, let alone after a long car journey.

> **There is often no better place for a child to discuss something on their mind than in the confines of the car, without eye contact and with the benefit of a clear chunk of your time.**

A car journey can be profitable time however as it's a chance to talk about the day and share any worries. There is often no better place for a child to discuss something on their mind than in the confines of the car, without eye contact and with the benefit of a clear chunk of your time.

Yet tiredness is a very important consideration. In the later prep years, the sheer time the journey takes has its impact on getting prep done in the evening, the timing for dinner and ultimately when the alarm needs to be set for the morning to ensure you get to school on time. The right choice of school needs to include the one where the logistics add up. If it takes too long to get there and back each day, you need to consider the impact this will have on your child.

If you live in a rural area, getting out the car will almost certainly be your only option. But if you live in a city, walking or cycling to school can provide a quicker and beneficial alternative. Yes, it rains from time to time (what's known as a 'character-forming opportunity') but as well as the considerable environmental benefit, your child arrives at school wide awake and ready for the day ahead. Compare if you will the children getting out of cars at the school gate, looking sleepy and tired, with those whose brains are already firing on all cylinders thanks to a cycle ride or walk to school? It's a consideration and, from personal experience, it doesn't actually chuck it down with rain at the precise moment you are cycling to or from school quite as much as you might first think.

Of course, the logistical challenge can be eased somewhat if you can opt for boarding and feel this is the right choice for your child. Parents have reinvented boarding. They turned their backs on the idea of sending their children away for a term at a time; parents worried about their children's welfare and wanted more regular contact while still giving them independence.

At the same time, schools adjusted to new financial realities. Many turned coeducational or opened their doors to day pupils. Termly boarding was now offered alongside weekly and flexi: a pick-and-mix option for busy parents, happy to pay for their child to stay at school just one or two nights a week. If you were a boarder thirty years ago, you will simply not recognise today's boarding environment.

The option of flexi-boarding is a popular choice in the latter years at some prep schools. It is seen as a good option for children wanting to increase their independence. For parents, especially those who are both working full-time, it opens up more flexibility during the week. For children, it provides excellent preparation for a senior school boarding environment, if that is where they are aiming. Many also argue that boarding can help the family dynamic.

Weekends are cherished time to spend together in fun or relaxing activities and without the stresses of the week, but only you know whether time apart from your children during the working week would result in better times together at weekends.

> Many also argue that boarding can help the family dynamic. Weekends are cherished time to spend together in activities and without the stresses of the week...

Of course, one of the major advantages of boarding for children is that they have access to the full range of facilities at the school outside of normal hours. It is no surprise that some of our best sportsmen and sportswomen have come from a boarding school background. Hours practising in the cricket nets, or out on the river, reap significant rewards. Pupils get to discover new interests and talents. Independent boarding schools are able to offer a whole host of extracurricular activities including music, drama and dance, as well as sporting interests.

All of this does come at an extraordinary financial cost however so it is an option only for a minority of families. If you can afford it, it will certainly change your weekly logistics.

> All of this does come at an extraordinary financial cost however so it is an option only for a minority of families. If you can afford it, it will certainly change your weekly logistics.

Opting for boarding doesn't negate the need to consider the distance to get to school however. Whilst not a daily commute, it will not be a termly journey either. There is a surprising number of events to which parents are invited and that ranges from sports fixtures to music concerts and drama performances. These add up, so in order to be able to support, you need to factor in the time for the events plus the logistics of getting to and from school.

Termly boarding can still require weekend collections, depending on the pattern of the school. Some schools might have a coach option but it all needs to be investigated and carefully considered.

Only you know your domestic arrangements and what's possible. But whatever you consider, don't underestimate the logistics; nor underestimate just how tired children get during the early years. It all adds up. And you need to get it right for everyone.

Practical aspects

Inspection reports

Perhaps the most important document you can read about an independent school is its inspection report. The process of inspection is complicated and can look impenetrable to parents; it is involved and often uses a lot of acronyms (be warned) but hang in there and the results are worth it.

Firstly, a bit of background to the process. Schools in membership of the Independent Schools Council (or ISC as it is known) in England are inspected by an organisation called the Independent Schools Inspectorate (ISI), appointed by the Department for Education (DfE).

Independent schools which are not in membership of ISC are inspected by Ofsted. ISC is an important organisation as it brings together seven associations of heads, bursars and governors. It therefore collectively represents over 1,400 independent schools, many of whom are well-known regionally and nationally.

Explaining inspections is quite complicated but one of the key things to understand is that schools are inspected to a framework. This ensures consistency between inspections and schools as well as being open

to scrutiny by all. At the heart of investigations is the extent to which schools are meeting the Independent School Standards (or 'The Education (Independent School Standards) Regulations 2014', which are set down in UK law) plus any other standards relevant to the school in question (such as the Early Years Foundation Stage or EYFS and any other standards, such as the National Minimum Standards for boarding, where appropriate).

Independent schools are inspected through what's known as a 'routine inspection' once every three years – with a maximum of two days' notice. Outside of these routine inspections, there are non-routine inspections which occur when schools change their registration (for example, altering the ages at which pupils join or leave the school), are subject to an inspection to monitor improvement having not met the standards previously, or if the DfE feel an urgent inspection is necessary. Inspections take place onsite and involve the whole school community, with inspectors wanting to talk to staff, pupils and parents, as well as the senior management and governors. Inspectors are experienced education professionals, trained for the role and ISI monitors the process and work of inspection teams. Parents can see the framework via the ISI website.

Once the inspection has concluded, the inspection team will then prepare a written report which – thanks to a consistent framework – will take the same format for each school. Parents can therefore compare and contrast where relevant. You will find the latest report for any school on its website, where it is obliged to make it available. You can also search for school reports via the Independent Schools Inspectorate (*www.isi.net*). The routine report will start with a 'summary of inspection findings' which gives you an overview. It then has five sections (ISI started a new framework in September 2023, so any inspections prior to this date will take the old format compared to that outlined here, but the differences are fairly self-explanatory).

The first section is concerned with leadership and management (the executive team, if you like, who deal with the day-to-day running of the school) and governance (the group of people who hire/fire the head and are ultimately responsible for the school). The second section is all about the quality of pupils' education and looks at progress and what the children achieve. The third is all about physical and mental health and how the emotional wellbeing of pupils is looked after at the school. The fourth is about careers provision and looks at the 'social and economic wellbeing and contribution to society'. Finally, the last section is on safeguarding and ensuring pupils are protected from harm and neglect.

On reading the report, you will get a clear understanding of where a school meets the standards. It is a slightly binary process in as much as the evaluation is between either meeting the standards or not – there are no ratings of 'good' or 'excellent'. If the inspection team do find any standards are not met, it will be in both the summary and relevant section of the report. Enforcement action through the DfE is a priority when multiple or serious failings are discovered. Do expect to see recommendations for next steps even on reports where all standards are met, or 'areas for action' in relation to any unmet standards.

The insight is to be gained by reading the text in detail and parents can then get a clear view of a school. If you have any questions about anything you read in a school's inspection report, do raise them with the school directly and seek their explanation.

As well as the education inspection reports, it is sensible for a parent to read up on the school's financial health. Many independent schools are registered charities and therefore submit an annual return to the Charity Commission each year. You can read this – and other background information about the charity – via the Commission's section on the *gov.uk* website. Here you will find details on governance, financial history and accounts. It makes for extensive reading and provides a comprehensive overview of a charity's last five financial periods. If a school is not a charity, and runs as a commercial company, you will instead be able to browse the publicly available information via the Companies House section on *gov.uk* and see past accounts.

There's a lot of information but it is important to understand the governance of any school you are considering. Far from being unimportant, the governors are ultimately responsible for the strategic direction and financial health of the organisation. You need to have confidence in their collective decision-making as they set the path for the long-term future.

Paying for it

There is no doubt that independent education is jaw-droppingly expensive and the cost continues to rise. One of the first mistakes parents can make when looking at the finances is to start doing the maths without taking into account annual price rises. It used to be that if you added a 5 per cent increase each year that would be more than sufficient. Those days are sadly long gone and it's no bad thing to ask a school for the fees from the last five years to give you a sense of the annual cost.

To be fair to schools, the cost increases are (usually) born from necessity. The major capital outlay for schools is staff – pupil ratios will be low and this is down to the number of staff, both teaching and support staff. In addition, even in prep schools, pupils will be taught by subject specialist teachers. Again, this pushes up the cost. There is then the myriad unsung heroes in a school which keep it running and yet often go unnoticed. The administration staff, from the Head's PA to the Admissions and HR team; the catering and facilities staff who ensure your child gets fed – and normally to an extremely good standard compared to the past – and keep the buildings clean, maintained and able to withstand the onslaught of careless pupils. And don't forget the grounds staff who ensure the upkeep of those wonderful playing fields, sports pitches and trees and flowers. Together, all these people, whose work often goes unnoticed by the pupils, are responsible for creating an environment which supports the best possible learning.

Practical aspects

And they all need to be paid and receive pensions. And finally, all these amazing facilities and buildings have a significant running cost which has an impact on fees. And that's before the latest plans for a new development.

So that helps explain why the fees are so high. Could they be lower? Well that's a debatable point. Excellent teaching doesn't need state-of-the-art facilities but it certainly makes it easier. Some school development plans could, in the cold light of day, be cut back and the 'frills and frippery' could be reined in sometimes. But it is a competitive market and parents have to realise their unwitting role in this. The financial realities of today's world may just temper some of the previous excesses of very large building projects.

Schools compete with each other in a number of areas but facilities is definitely one of them. Performing arts centres, sixth form buildings, state-of-the-art sports complexes – these are common features of the senior school landscape. Prep schools are not far behind and, given the choice, parents will often opt for a school with very strong facilities. And so there is inevitable competition whether schools mean to or not. Ultimately, parents pay for all this and it drives up the cost.

You also need to factor in the hidden costs. Uniform, sports kit, trips and expeditions plus music or drama lessons, as well as other enrichment activities – these all add up to a considerable additional amount on the termly bill. To make the hours work, you might also be paying for after-care or another club, so you can collect your child a little later in the day. And don't forget the logistics – is there a school bus and what is the cost? If not, what is the cost to get to school each day in the car – or can you cycle or walk?

> **And don't forget the logistics – is there a school bus and what is the cost?**

How you finance the cost of fees is very much a personal problem. Often grandparents are contributing or parents have moved house and used the proceeds of a property sale to offset the cost. For parents who cannot afford the fees, most schools offer bursaries and financial support. They don't want the fees to be a barrier and parents should not be put off from starting a discussion regarding bursaries. But to be clear, bursaries are only offered for genuine need and application is an intrusive process.

If you have assets or expenses which can be cut back first, this will be suggested prior to any bursary being offered.

One sensible option is to calculate the full cost over all the school years; then work out a yearly average and start 'overpaying' into a savings account to soften the blow later. Early years at prep is much cheaper and the time to save. Don't feel you are alone if the cost feels very expensive and will be a struggle: the majority of independent school parents are making massive financial sacrifices to afford the fees. They make the choice to forgo holidays, new cars or bigger houses to give their children what they feel is the right schooling for their needs. And don't be shy to discuss the finances with the school. Bursary options may be appropriate for your needs and it is always worth discussing the options. Bursaries certainly carry no stigma; they are a golden ticket for your child. If you cannot afford the fees, apply for a bursary and let your child access a wonderful education.

One solution which some parents consider is to delay independent schooling until their child is 11, opting for the local primary school and perhaps tutoring to assist with entrance exams. Whilst obviously an option, there is much more to the prep school years than simply to gain a ticket to progress to senior school. The scope and scale of the taught and untaught curriculum is enormous – and the opportunities for the extra-curricular can rarely be replicated.

Indeed, many a prep school pupil on leaving in Year 8 could sit GCSEs in the key subjects and score remarkably well for their age. They have learnt how to learn, how to approach examinations and are very well prepared. Many would argue that if you had to make a choice, it would be to opt for prep school fees and then switch into the state sector if cost becomes prohibitive for a private secondary school. Yes, it's a difficult move but when considered just from a child's academic progression, it is compelling. And if you live in an area with excellent state grammar schools on your doorstep, you are very fortunate indeed.

Fees are eye-wateringly expensive but one thing to remember is that just because parents opt to send their child to a private school does not mean they are wealthy.

Other considerations

Independent schools are the inheritors of a lot of history. And whilst in many cases that's a positive thing, it can create a barrier of terminology at best – and appear detached at worst. Because of this position, they are also associated with many unhelpful myths, stereotypes and undeserved labels. Let's try and shake off a few and correct some others.

First up, what is the difference between an 'independent school', a 'private school' and a 'public school'? Well, in essence, the answer is actually nothing; they are the same thing. Historically, a 'public school' was a subset of schools which were the subject of the Clarendon Commission report in the 1860s but in today's world, the terms are completely interchangeable. The media (and some politicians) tend to use 'private' and 'public' depending on the story but it often has a negative connotation. Nothing says posh, elitist and privileged more than 'public school' so it has largely become an unhelpful label. Private schools, on the other hand, prefer to use the term 'independent school' as it epitomises what they are all about.

But when we talk about 'independent', what do we actually mean? Julie Robinson, Chief Executive of the Independent Schools' Council, summed it up well in an article for *Attain*: 'For 'independent', read 'free-thinking' because these schools, free from state control, can design their own timetables, choose their own exam systems, build on values and a culture that suits local needs. They defy stereotyping. There is a wide range of character amongst independent schools, just as there is among children.' [8]

> **Transition from one school to another, with the pressure of exams, is a daunting process for both pupils and parents but leaving one school and making friends at another provides valuable life lessons.**

Another area of difference between the state and independent sectors is the terms 'junior' and 'senior'. The primary years are usually referred to as 'junior', 'preparatory' or 'prep' and cover the period from Reception through until Year 6 or Year 8 (11 or 13 years) at which point pupils transition to 'senior school' or 'secondary' as it is otherwise known. Traditionally, girls prep schools ended at 11 and boys at 13; today, many co-ed preps go up to 13 years and so there has been a blurring of the age at which pupils change schools. Some schools are part of a larger foundation, whereby pupils can join at nursery age and progress through the school until leaving at age 18. This makes transition easier as it doesn't involve leaving the school. For some parents this provides a continuity and reassurance but it does presuppose that the decision you make at an early age is the right one for a child who has yet to develop an aptitude in any particular area.

Transition from one school to another, with the pressure of exams, is a daunting process for both pupils and parents but leaving one school and making friends at another provides valuable life lessons. Change is inevitable and learning to be comfortable with it – and to adapt to whatever it may bring – stands you in good stead for the future. Much depends on the choices you make from the options available and no route is necessarily better; it all depends on what is right for your child.

Another source of ambiguity is that of scholarships and bursaries. Scholarships have nothing to do with bursaries, with the latter being the route through which parents can seek fee remission, subject to the level of their earnings. It's the way that extraordinary educational opportunities can be opened up to children from backgrounds who would otherwise not be able to afford the fees.

Bursaries are transformative and, whilst the sector has done much to expand and support the provision of them, more should be done to open up the privilege of a private education beyond just those who can afford it. Sadly, the economic climate, coupled with the storm clouds generated by Labour's VAT policy, risks bursary provision going backwards rather than expanding.

In contrast to bursaries, scholarships are a recognition of a pupil's ability in a particular field. They were traditionally reserved for academic pursuits, music and art but many senior schools offer a much wider range. They don't usually have a fee reduction attached – or if they do it is a token – as fee reductions should always be means-tested and scholarships are not. Scholarships do unfortunately look outdated in today's education climate and cause frustration at prep schools due to each senior school having its own exam and timetable for assessment. This creates additional work for prep schools, preparing pupils for different exams at different times of the year.

> **Sadly, the economic climate, coupled with the storm clouds generated by Labour's VAT policy, risks bursary provision going backwards rather than expanding.**

More fundamental is the problem of giving a scholarship to a pupil at entrance rather than after the first year at senior school, when they have settled in and demonstrated their abilities. As Dr Tim Hands wrote in a personal comment piece in *Attain*: 'A scholarship given to the wrong person is a label many a scholar would rather have been without. This means that too many pupils find themselves the inheritors of a set of unhelpful expectations. In short, too many scholars become pupils with glorious futures behind them.'[9]

Dr Hands summed up the problem of scholarships thus: 'Scholarships are a cross between an institutional virility test and a sales incentive. They are unhelpful for all concerned. Surely one day, the scholarship boards in prep schools will look as outdated as the Oxbridge honours boards in many a senior school. Prep school heads will increasingly focus on the proud achievements of all – how many pupils get into their first choice of senior school – rather than there being a subset memorialised and singled out for unhelpful adulation.' [9]

> **Without doubt the biggest myth and misconception about independent schools is the notion that you must be wealthy to send your child to a private school.**

In the decade since Dr Hands wrote these comments, little has changed. Whilst some scholarships are awarded later, many schools still offer scholarships at entrance. And until this changes, parents need to continue to accept the confused and outdated system. Before your son or daughter embarks on a scholarship, do make sure it is the right decision and will not cause undue pressure later.

Without doubt the biggest myth and misconception about independent schools is the notion that you must be wealthy to send your child to a private school. It's from a blinkered view that because the fees are high, everyone attending them must have parents who can easily afford the cost. It ignores the much more complex picture of how some parents find the money – including through multiple jobs, remortgaging, downsizing, contributions from grandparents and huge belt-tightening.

Making decisions

Open days and admissions

I hope that by now we have covered all the key factors to think about when choosing a school. Some might be obvious but others require a lot more thought and you may be wrestling with a few dilemmas. How do you compare one school with another when they appear to offer something very similar?

The first thing to do is to start drawing up a shortlist. And this list needs to give a score or weighting based on your criteria. You may want to draw a series of columns and list each in turn. They can include: co-ed/single sex, the Head, pastoral care, extracurricular, inspection and financial due diligence, and of course, the logistics of the journey to/from school. Give each one a tick/cross or a score out of 10 from what you have been able to research. Fairly quickly, you will be able to discount some schools as not fitting your needs. Have a look at those headings again and see if there are any about which you are uncertain.

Of course, at this stage it might be hard to have particularly strong feelings about say the Head, unless you have met her or him already. That's where the visit – or Open Day – will come in but at this stage, all you are doing is working out what might, in theory, be an

option. There is no point going to an Open Day at a school if it logistically doesn't stack up. With your list complete, check out when each school is having its next open event or if they encourage individual visits.

> One dilemma is whether to visit schools for an Open Day or a personal tour. Both have their merits and schools tend to offer a wide range of opportunities.

One dilemma is whether to visit schools for an Open Day or a personal tour. Both have their merits and schools tend to offer a wide range of opportunities. Open Days can provide a more sanitised view with all the best things on display and some areas might be off-limits. But you will usually have a pupil as a tour guide who will provide a fascinating insight into the areas of school life they enjoy. Children tend to provide a warts-and-all commentary and are very honest in their opinions. Don't forget to ask about food. As ever, it is in the margins where you get the greatest insight. At one Open Day, I left a building down the wrong corridor by mistake, walking past some classrooms which were not part of the main event for parents. A group of pupils were messing about, one was lying on a table and the others were throwing a paper ball around, laughing and chatting. As I paused, they quickly stopped, smiled and said a cheery hello. Unscripted, honest and genuine: it told me this was a happy school. Look for the margins, those opportunities to get an insight beyond the polished Open Day.

A personal tour can, on face value, offer you more than an Open Day as you can choose exactly what you want to see. It will also take place on a normal school day without special classroom sessions or activities taking place. But you will also be steered in a particular direction and might need to work harder to get your own insight. But remember that whatever you think, your child will have a strong and valuable opinion which may well differ from your own.

Compare notes carefully when you get home and dig out that shortlist again. Do you still agree with the scores you gave previously? Add your child's views into the mix and see what happens. After you have been to several Open Days you

Making decisions

should start to see a clear picture of what you both like and where your future direction might be.

The next stage, if your child is already at a prep school and you are looking at senior schools, is to talk it all through with the prep school head. Are your conclusions in line with his or her feelings of future direction? If not, discuss it and try to understand why this might be – and keep an open mind. We have talked in detail about the need to ensure the right fit; you cannot mould a child to suit a school however much you (or your child) might want it to work.

> …you cannot mould a child to suit a school however much you (or your child) might want it to work.

The final part is to look carefully through the Admissions details. You will need to register for a place, normally paying a fee at this stage to join, and then wait for the next stage. The school's website will outline the process in detail but, if you have any questions, do contact the admissions team who will be pleased to help you.

For many senior schools, there will be an entrance examination to sit and usually an interview. Over-preparation is not a good idea for any admissions interview and, much like schools can spot tutoring, the over-prepared child does not sit comfortably at interview.

As a parent, you have done your part. You now just need to support and encourage.

Attain Guide 2025

Taking the long view

There is no doubt that choosing a school for your child – and especially the process of changing school – can quickly become pressured, stressful and difficult. Hopefully, the advice in this book helps to make the process a little easier but, as parents, we can sometimes end up too involved; although easy to say, it is the time to step back and remember the bigger picture.

Over my years as an education editor, I read a lot of advice from Headteachers. One of the best was a piece written by Peter Tait, who was Headmaster of Sherborne Preparatory School in Dorset for 17 years. He wrote an article for *Attain* entitled *Ten Observations for Parents* [10] and it helps put everything discussed in this book into perspective:

1. *Don't be in such a hurry.* It does not help to push children before they are emotionally and physically ready. They will develop at different stages, so

don't constantly compare them with others; instead enjoy them as they are.

2. Confidence and self-belief have to be grown, not bestowed.
Parents should have high expectations for their children, but they must be realistic. Children can be best helped by being encouraged to work hard, to be more adventurous and to enjoy their achievements, however small.

3. Presentation of work and self are very important, even in an age of computers.
Pride in work and dress, clarity of thought and expression as well as good manners are vital components of becoming successful and fulfilled human beings – and begin at home.

4. Children need structure and discipline in their lives.
Being organised is vital in work and leisure, yet more and more children cannot manage their day or their possessions. Agree some rules and stick by them, but try also to inculcate the value of self-discipline and of managing time well.

5. Don't make excuses for your children.
Work with schools and teachers, not against them. If you don't respect your children's teacher, nor will your children. Trust your schools and treat your teachers as professionals. They know your children in a way you cannot.

6. Help them grow a moral compass.
Teach them right from wrong, but also the importance of being part of the whole, of thinking of others, of kindness, honesty and similar traits. Ethics and values are in danger of being swamped by the rapidity of progress and, again, need to come from home.

7. Be techno-savvy.
Terrifying to some, the exciting reality is that your children inhabit a virtual world as well as the physical world. The downside of the technological revolution is that it comes with lots of doors into dangerous and unsavoury places. Talk about technology with your children and keep computers in communal places in the home – never bedrooms. Learn from them (but don't stalk them), and do hammer on about values and ethics and social and personal responsibility in the choices they make.

8. Children need to learn to cope on their own.
Having a specific learning difficulty, for instance, may be a challenge, but it can also prove

a strength in the long-term if it teaches the child to engage with learning and become a resilient learner. A good attitude, resilience and a healthy work ethic are the keys to success.

9. *Be realistic for your children and don't judge them by your educational experience.*
Chances are they are already operating on a different plane. Nor should you be obsessed with keeping them busy all the time – you are raising a child not filling in a curriculum vitae. They will do better if encouraged, rather than being force-fed.

10. *Be a parent and a role model first and a friend second.*
Your child's achievements at prep school need to be seen in the context of the longevity of the journey. Your job is to nurture and support your child so he or she becomes independent and able to move on, not peak too soon. Guide them with their homework, but don't do it for them! Engender a love of reading, for that is invaluable. And always focus on the joy, the privilege of learning.

from 'Ten Observations for Parents' by Peter Tait, Attain, 2015.

The purpose of this book is to make the difficult and challenging task of choosing a school for your child – at whatever age – easier. If it has shined a light on a hidden aspect or helped you to look again at an issue, we have hopefully succeeded in this aim.

As Editor of *Attain* for 15 years, I was incredibly fortunate to meet so many amazing headteachers and work closely with some brilliant contributors including Peter Tait, Tim Hands and Julie Robinson. *Attain's* readers benefited enormously from their regular articles. This book was born out of those years of being an education editor. It's a collective distilling of all I have learnt in the hope that other parents find it of use.

Parenting is hard and nobody can make decisions for you. There are no shortcuts or quick fixes. But you know your wonderful child and you know what makes him or her happy.

And that must be your guide.

Schools' Directory

Our Schools' Directory contains some of the leading independent schools in the country. I hesitate to use the phrase 'best schools' as I have been at pains throughout this book to make clear that parents should not seek out the 'best' but rather the 'right' school for their child. When searching for the right school however, it helps if it's from a selection of schools which – by a wide-range of criteria – represent some of the foremost in the country.

These schools have a clear commitment to excellence in a number of areas: academic achievement, extra curricular provision, pastoral care and more. All schools in our Directory are in membership of one or more of the leading Heads' associations which form part of the Independent Schools Council. For a Head to join these associations requires a commitment to ensuring excellence across all aspects of their school and maintaining the very highest standards.

These schools recognise the critical importance of staff professional development, enabling them to deliver innovation in teaching and inspire the pupils in their care. They also value the importance of being part of a wider community and are engaged in significant partnership and community outreach programmes.

As leading independent schools, they provide an excellent education but one which comes at a significant financial cost. They recognise that this is beyond the reach of many parents and so provide bursaries and financial support to enable them to offer a life-changing education to a child.

We do not rank or compare schools in our Directory. Schools cannot pay to be included – we list simply on merit. Some schools support our work through advertising; their listings are highlighted and profile photos are also included for some. We are very grateful for their support over the years and helping ensure our success.

QR codes are provided so you can jump to a particular regional page on our website. For details about an individual school, you can enter the Quick Link code – a four digit code which you simply type into your browser after our website address – e.g. *attain.guide/a98s* – and you will jump directly to that school's profile page.

Attain Guide 2025

London

Use the QR code to learn more about schools in London

East London

City of London School	Boys, 10-18	Day	Queen Victoria Street, EC4V 3AL	c23a
City of London School for Girls	Girls, 7-18	Day	Barbican, EC2Y 8BB	c88b
Forest School	Boys & Girls, 4-18	Day	Snaresbrook, E17 3PY	f13p
Gatehouse School	Boys & Girls, 3-11	Day	Sewardstone Road, E2 9JG	g89j
St Paul's Cathedral School	Boys & Girls, 4-13	Day & Boarding	New Change, EC4M 9AD	s89a

North London

School	Pupils	Type	Location	Code
Avenue Pre-Prep & Nursery School	Boys & Girls, 3-7	Day	Highgate, N6 5RX	a85r
Channing School	Girls, 4-18	Day	Highgate, N6 5HF	c15h
Grange Park Prep School	Boys & Girls, 3-11	Day	Grange Park, N21 2EA	g62e
Highgate School	Boys & Girls, 4-18	Day	Highgate, N6 4AY	h94a
Keble Prep	Boys & Girls, 3-13	Day	Winchmore Hill, N21 1BG	k01b
Kerem School	Boys & Girls, 3-11	Day	Norrice Lea, N2 0RE	k80r
North Bridge House Senior	Boys & Girls, 11-18	Day	Islington, N1 2NQ	n32n
Palmers Green High School	Girls, 3-16	Day	Hoppers Road, N21 3LJ	p53l
Salcombe Preparatory School	Boys & Girls, 3-11	Day	Green Road, N14 4AD	s94a
Vita et Pax School	Boys & Girls, 3-11	Day	Southgate, N14 4AT	v44a

North West London

Abercorn School	Boys & Girls, 2-16	Day	Abercorn Place, NW8 9XP	a99x
Alpha Preparatory School	Boys & Girls, 3-11	Day	Harrow, HA1 1SH	a51s
Arnold House School	Boys, 3-13	Day	St John's Wood, NW8 0LH	a60l
Belmont Mill Hill Prep	Boys & Girls, 7-13	Day	Mill Hill, NW7 4ED	b24e
Buckingham Preparatory School	Boys, 3-11	Day	Pinner, HA5 5DT	b85d
Devonshire House Prep School	Boys 3-13, Girls 3-11	Day	Hampstead, NW3 6AE	d26a
Francis Holland, Regent's Park	Girls, 11-18	Day	Ivor Place, NW1 6XR	f06x
Grimsdell Mill Hill Pre-Prep	Boys & Girls, 3-7	Day	Mill Hill, NW7 1QR	g31q
Harrow School	Boys, 13-18	Boarding	Harrow on the Hill, HA1 3HP	h93h
Hendon Preparatory School	Boys & Girls, 3-11	Day	Hendon, NW4 1TD	h11t
Hereward House School	Boys, 4-13	Day	Hampstead, NW3 4NY	h94n
Holland House School	Boys & Girls, 4-11	Day	Edgware, HA8 8TP	h78t

Schools' Directory

Ivy House School	Boys & Girls, 2-11	Day	North End Road, NW11 7SX	i97s
Merchant Taylors' School	Boys, 11-18	Day	Northwood, HA6 2HT	m72h
Mill Hill School	Boys & Girls, 13-18	Day & Boarding	Mill Hill Village, NW7 1QS	m71q
Naima Jewish Preparatory School	Boys & Girls, 2-11	Day	Andover Road, NW6 5ED	n05e
North Bridge House Pre-Prep	Boys & Girls, 2-7	Day	Hampstead, NW3 5JY	n55j
North Bridge House Prep School	Boys & Girls, 4-13	Day	Gloucester Avenue, NW1 7AB	n47a
North London Collegiate School	Girls, 4-18	Day	Edgware, HA8 7RJ	n87r
Northwood College for Girls	Girls, 3-18	Day	Northwood, HA6 2YE	n82y
Orley Farm School	Boys & Girls, 4-13	Day	Harrow on the Hill, HA1 3NU	o73n
Quainton Hall School	Boys & Girls, 3-11	Day	Harrow, HA1 1RX	q61r
Reddiford School	Boys & Girls, 3-11	Day	Pinner, HA5 5HH	r15h
Saint Christina's School	Boys & Girls, 3-11	Day	Regents Park, NW8 7PY	s07p
Sarum Hall School	Girls, 3-11	Day	Hampstead, NW3 3EL	s03e
South Hampstead High School	Girls, 4-18	Day	Maresfield Gardens, NW3 5SS	s75s
St Anthony's School for Boys	Boys, 2-13	Day	Hampstead, NW3 6NP	s06n
St Christopher's Hampstead	Girls, 4-11	Day	Belsize Lane, NW3 5AE	s95a
St Helen's School	Girls, 3-18	Day	Northwood, HA6 3AS	s73a
St John's School	Boys, 3-13	Day	Northwood, HA6 3QY	s63q
St Margaret's School Hampstead	Girls, 4-16	Day	Hampstead, NW3 7SR	s07s
St Martin's School Northwood	Boys, 3-13	Day	Northwood, HA6 2DJ	s92d
St Mary's School Hampstead	Girls, 2-11	Day	Hampstead, NW3 6PG	s26p
The Cavendish School	Girls, 3-11	Day	Inverness Street, NW1 7HB	t67h
The Hall School	Boys, 4-13	Day	Hampstead, NW3 4NU	t64n
The John Lyon School	Boys & Girls, 11-18	Day	Harrow, HA2 0HN	t90h
University College School	Boys 4-18, Girls 16-18	Day	Hampstead, NW3 6XH	u46x

Alleyn's School
Day · Boys & Girls, 4-18 · Dulwich, SE22 8SU

Eltham College
Day · Boys & Girls, 7-18 · Grove Park Road, SE9 4QF

South East London

Alleyn's School	Boys & Girls, 4-18	Day	Dulwich, SE22 8SU	a98s
Blackheath High School	Girls, 3-18	Day	Blackheath, SE3 7AG	b17a
Blackheath Prep	Boys & Girls, 3-11	Day	Blackheath, SE3 0NJ	b60n
Bromley High School	Girls, 4-18	Day	Bromley, BR1 2TW	b02t
Colfe's School	Boys & Girls, 3-18	Day	Horn Park Lane, SE12 8AW	c58a
DLD College London	Boys & Girls, 13-19	Day & Boarding	Westminster Bridge Rd, SE1 7FX	d87f
Dulwich College	Boys 2-18, Girls 2-7	Day & Boarding	Dulwich Common, SE21 7LD	d07l
Dulwich Prep London	Boys 3-13, Girls 3-5	Day	Dulwich, SE21 7AA	d47a
Eltham College	**Boys & Girls, 7-18**	**Day**	**Grove Park Road, SE9 4QF**	**e14q**
James Allen's Girls' School	Girls, 4-18	Day	East Dulwich Grove, SE22 8TE	j98t
Oakfield Preparatory School	Boys & Girls, 2-11	Day	Dulwich, SE21 8HP	o78h
Rosemead Preparatory School	Boys & Girls, 3-11	Day	Thurlow Park Road, SE21 8HZ	r18h
St Dunstan's College	Boys & Girls, 4-18	Day	Catford, SE6 4TY	s04t
St Olave's Prep School	Boys & Girls, 3-11	Day	New Eltham, SE9 3QS	s83q
Sydenham High School	**Girls, 4-18**	**Day**	**Westwood Hill, SE26 6BL**	**s86b**

Sydenham High School
Day · Girls, 4-18 · Westwood Hill, SE26 6BL

Lady Eleanor Holles School
Day · Girls, 7-18 · Hampton, TW12 3HF

South West London

Brighton College Prep Kensington	Boys & Girls, 2-13	Day	Prince's Gardens, SW7 1ND	p51n
Broomwood Prep Boys	Boys, 3-13	Day	Wandsworth, SW11 6EL	n96e
Broomwood Prep Girls	Girls, 3-13	Day	Wandsworth, SW12 8NR	b28n
Cameron Vale	Boys & Girls, 4-11	Day	The Vale, SW3 4AD	c94a
Croydon High School	Girls, 3-18	Day	South Croydon, CR2 8YB	c18y
Donhead	Boys & Girls, 3-11	Day	Wimbledon, SW19 4NP	d04n
Eaton House Belgravia	Boys, 2-11	Day	Eaton Gate, SW1W 9BA	e39b

Schools' Directory

Eaton House The Manor	Boys 2-13, Girls 2-11	Day	Clapham Northside, SW4 9RU	e59r
Eaton Square Prep School	Boys & Girls, 2-11	Day	Eccleston Square, SW1V 1PP	e81p
Emanuel School	Boys & Girls, 10-18	Day	Battersea Rise, SW11 1HS	e01h
Falcons School	Boys & Girls, 2-11	Day	Putney, SW15 6PY	f76p
Finton House School	Boys & Girls, 4-11	Day	Trinity Road, SW17 7HL	f37h
Francis Holland, Sloane Square	Girls, 4-18	Day	Graham Terrace, SW1W 8JF	f48j
Garden House School	Boys & Girls, 3-11	Day	Turks Row, SW3 4TW	g04t
Glendower Preparatory School	Girls, 3-11	Day	Kensington, SW7 5JX	g65j
Halliford School	Boys 11-18, Girls 16-18	Day	Shepperton, TW17 9HX	h99h
Hampton Pre-Prep & Prep	Boys 3-11, Girls 3-7	Day	Hampton, TW12 2LP	h82l
Hampton School	Boys, 11-18	Day	Hampton, TW12 3HD	h43h
Hornsby House School	Boys & Girls, 4-11	Day	Hearnville Road, SW12 8RS	h48r
Hurlingham School	Boys & Girls, 2-11	Day	Putney Bridge Road, SW15 2NQ	h32n
Ibstock Place School	Boys & Girls, 4-18	Day	Roehampton, SW15 5PY	i45p
Kensington Prep School	Girls, 4-11	Day	Fulham Road, SW6 5PA	k25p
Kew College	Boys & Girls, 3-11	Day	Kew, TW9 3HQ	k93h
Kew Green Preparatory School	Boys & Girls, 4-11	Day	Kew Green, TW9 3AF	k53a
Kew House School	Boys & Girls, 11-18	Day	Capital Interchange Way, TW8 0EX	k10e
King's College School Wimbledon	Boys 7-18, Girls 16-18	Day	Wimbledon Common, SW19 4TT	k14t
King's House School	Boys & Girls, 3-13	Day	Richmond, TW10 6ES	k66e
Knightsbridge School	Boys & Girls, 3-16	Day	Pont Street, SW1X 0BD	k50b
Lady Eleanor Holles School	**Girls, 7-18**	**Day**	**Hampton, TW12 3HF**	t33h
More House School	Girls, 11-18	Day	Chelsea, SW1X 0AA	m40a
Newland House School	Boys & Girls, 3-13	Day	Twickenham, TW1 4TQ	n74t
Newton Prep	Boys & Girls, 3-13	Day	Battersea Park Rd, SW8 4BX	n94b
Parsons Green Prep	Boys & Girls, 4-11	Day	Fulham Park Road, SW6 4LJ	p24l
Prospect House School	Boys & Girls, 3-11	Day	Putney Hill, SW15 3NT	p93n
Putney High School	Girls, 4-18	Day	Putney Hill, SW15 6BH	p76b
Queen's Gate School	Girls, 4-18	Day	Kensington, SW7 5LE	q75l
St Catherine's School, Twickenham	Girls, 3-18	Day	Twickenham, TW1 4QJ	s84q
St Paul's School	Boys, 7-18	Day & Boarding	Barnes, SW13 9JT	s39j
Staines Preparatory School	**Boys & Girls, 3-11**	**Day**	**Staines, TW18 2BT**	s72b
Streatham & Clapham High School	Girls, 3-18	Day	Streatham Hill, SW16 1AW	s51a
Sussex House	Boys, 8-13	Day	Cadogan Square, SW1X 0EA	s70e
Sutton High School	Girls, 3-18	Day	Sutton, SM1 2AX	s22a

The Mall School	Boys & Girls, 0-11	Day	Twickenham, TW2 5NQ	t25n
The Old Vicarage School	Girls, 3-11	Day	Richmond-upon-Thames, TW10 6QX	t46q
The Rowans School	Boys & Girls, 3-7	Day	Wimbledon, SW20 0EG	t10e
The Study Preparatory School	Girls, 4-11	Day	Wimbledon Village, SW19 5ER	t95e
Thomas's Battersea	Boys & Girls, 4-11	Day	Battersea High Street, SW11 3JB	t93j
Thomas's Clapham	Boys & Girls, 4-13	Day	Broomwood Road, SW11 6JZ	t96j
Thomas's Fulham	Boys & Girls, 4-11	Day	Hugon Road, SW6 3ES	t33e
Tower House School	Boys, 4-13	Day	East Sheen, SW14 8LF	t28l
Twickenham Preparatory School	Boys & Girls, 4-11	Day	Hampton, TW12 2SA	t32s
Unicorn School	Boys & Girls, 3-11	Day	Richmond, TW9 3JX	u03j
Ursuline Preparatory School	Girls 4-11, Boys 3-4	Day	Wimbledon, SW20 8HR	u08h
Westminster Abbey Choir School	Boys, 8-13	Boarding	Westminster, SW1P 3NY	w13n
Westminster Cathedral Choir Sch.	Boys, 4-13	Day & Boarding	Westminster, SW1P 1QH	w21q
Westminster School	Boys & Girls, 13-18	Day & Boarding	Westminster, SW1P 3PB	w13p
Westminster Under School	Boys & Girls, 4-13	Day	Vincent Square, SW1P 2NN	w62n
Whitgift School	Boys, 10-18	Day	South Croydon, CR2 6YT	w36y
Willington School	Boys & Girls, 3-11	Day	Wimbledon, SW19 7QQ	w77q
Wimbledon Common Prep School	Boys, 4-7	Day	Wimbledon, SW19 4TA	w64t
Wimbledon High School	Girls, 4-18	Day	Wimbledon, SW19 4AB	w14a

South West London — s72b

Staines Preparatory School
Day · Boys & Girls, 3-11 · Staines, TW18 2BT

West London — s22e

St Benedict's School
Day · Boys & Girls, 3-18 · Ealing, W5 2ES

West London

attain.guide/d72d

Avenue House School	Boys & Girls, 4-11	Day	Ealing, W13 8LS	a78l
Bassett House School	Boys & Girls, 3-11	Day	Kensington, W10 6JP	b56j
Bute House Prep School	Girls, 4-11	Day	Hammersmith, W6 7EA	b97e
Chiswick & Bedford Park Prep	Girls 3-11, Boys 3-7	Day	Chiswick, W4 1TX	c21t

Schools' Directory

School	Type	Day/Boarding	Location	Code
Durston House School	**Boys & Girls, 3-13**	**Day**	**Ealing, W5 2DR**	d72d
Godolphin and Latymer School	Girls, 11-18	Day	Hammersmith, W6 0PG	g50p
Latymer Upper School	Boys & Girls, 7-18	Day	King Street, W6 9LR	l69l
Maida Vale School	Boys & Girls, 11-18	Day	Saltram Crescent, W9 3HR	m33h
Norland Place School	Boys & Girls, 4-11	Day	Holland Park, W11 4UH	n74u
Notting Hill & Ealing High School	Girls, 4-18	Day	Cleveland Road, W13 8AX	n88a
Notting Hill Preparatory School	Boys & Girls, 4-13	Day	Lancaster Road, W11 1QQ	n71q
Orchard House School	Boys & Girls, 3-11	Day	Newton Grove, W4 1LB	o51l
Pembridge Hall School	Girls, 4-11	Day	Notting Hill Gate, W2 4EH	p74e
Queen's College London	Girls, 4-18	Day	Harley Street, W1G 8BT	q58b
Ravenscourt Park Prep School	Boys & Girls, 4-11	Day	Chiswick, W6 0SL	r20s
Royal Ballet School	Boys & Girls, 11-19	Day & Boarding	Covent Garden, WC2E 9DA	r09d
St Augustine's Priory	Girls, 3-18	Day	Ealing, W5 2JL	s82j
St Benedict's School	**Boys & Girls, 3-18**	**Day**	**Ealing, W5 2ES**	s22e
St Helen's College	Boys & Girls, 2-11	Day	Hillingdon, UB10 9JX	s79j
St James Preparatory School	Boys & Girls, 2-11	Day	Earsby Street, W14 8SH	s08s
St James Senior Girls' School	Girls, 11-18	Day	Earsby Street, W14 8SH	s78s
St Paul's Girls' School	Girls, 11-18	Day	Brook Green, W6 7BS	s07b
Thomas's Kensington	Boys & Girls, 4-11	Day	Cottesmore Gardens, W8 5PR	t65p
Wetherby Preparatory School	Boys, 8-13	Day	Bryanston Square, W1H 2EA	w82e
Wetherby School	Boys, 3-8	Day	Pembridge Square, W2 4ED	w64e
Wetherby Senior School	Boys, 11-18	Day	Marylebone Lane, W1U 2QB	w42q

Discover more about schools listed in the Schools' Directory by using the quick link code to jump to the page on our website, e.g. *attain.guide/s22e*

Attain Guide 2025

South East

Use the QR code to learn more about schools in the South East

Berkshire

↗ attain.guide/c28l

School	Pupils	Type	Location	Code
Bradfield College	Boys & Girls, 13-18	Day & Boarding	Reading, RG7 6AU	↗ b56a
Brockhurst & Marlston House	Boys & Girls, 3-13	Day & Boarding	Newbury, RG18 9UL	↗ b29u
Cheam School	**Boys & Girls, 3-13**	**Day & Boarding**	**Newbury, RG19 8LD**	↗ **c28l**
Claires Court Schools	Boys & Girls, 2-18	Day	Maidenhead, SL6 6AW	↗ c86a
Crosfields School	Boys & Girls, 3-16	Day	Reading, RG2 9BL	↗ c19b
Dolphin School	Boys & Girls, 3-13	Day	Reading, RG10 0FR	↗ d40f
Downe House School	**Girls, 11-18**	**Day & Boarding**	**Thatcham, RG18 9JJ**	↗ **d89j**
Eagle House	Boys & Girls, 3-13	Day & Boarding	Sandhurst, GU47 8PH	↗ e38p
Elstree School	Boys & Girls, 3-13	Day & Boarding	Reading, RG7 5TD	↗ e55t
Eton College	Boys, 13-18	Boarding	Windsor, SL4 6DW	↗ e76d
Eton End School	Boys & Girls, 3-11	Day	Datchet, SL3 9AX	↗ e99a
Heathfield School	**Girls, 11-18**	**Day & Boarding**	**Ascot, SL5 8BQ**	↗ **h18b**
Herries School	Boys & Girls, 2-11	Day	Maidenhead, SL6 9BD	↗ h59b
Highfield Prep School	Girls 3-11, Boys 3-7	Day	Maidenhead, SL6 1PD	↗ h41p
Holme Grange School	Boys & Girls, 2-16	Day	Wokingham, RG40 3AL	↗ h23a
Horris Hill	Boys & Girls, 2-13	Day & Boarding	Newbury, RG20 9DJ	↗ h99d
Lambrook	Boys & Girls, 3-13	Day & Boarding	Ascot, RG42 6LU	↗ l06l
Leighton Park School	Boys & Girls, 11-18	Day & Boarding	Reading, RG2 7ED	↗ l27e
Luckley House School	Boys & Girls, 11-18	Day & Boarding	Wokingham, RG40 3EU	↗ l93e
Ludgrove School	Boys, 8-13	Day & Boarding	Wokingham, RG40 3AB	↗ l13a
LVS Ascot	Boys & Girls, 4-18	Day & Boarding	Ascot, SL5 8DR	↗ l08d

Cheam School
Day · Boys & Girls, 3-13 · Newbury, RG19 8LD

Heathfield School
Day · Girls, 11-18 · Ascot, SL5 8BQ

Schools' Directory

Berkshire — s47d

St George's Ascot
Day · Girls, 11-18 · Ascot, SL5 7DZ

Berkshire — w57p

Wellington College
Day · Boys & Girls, 13-18 · Crowthorne, RG45 7PU

School	Pupils	Type	Location	Code
Pangbourne College	Boys & Girls, 11-18	Day & Boarding	Reading, RG8 8LA	p78l
Papplewick	Boys, 7-13	Day & Boarding	Ascot, SL5 7LH	p97l
Queen Anne's School	*Girls, 11-18*	*Day & Boarding*	**Reading, RG4 6DX**	q26d
Reading Blue Coat School	Boys & Girls, 11-18	Day	Sonning, RG4 6SU	r36s
Reddam House	Boys & Girls, 0-18	Day & Boarding	Wokingham, RG41 5BG	r55b
St Andrew's Berkshire	Boys & Girls, 3-13	Day & Boarding	Pangbourne, RG8 8QA	s18q
St Bernard's Preparatory School	Boys & Girls, 2-11	Day	Slough, SL1 1TB	s51t
St Edward's Prep Reading	Boys & Girls, 3-11	Day	Reading, RG30 2JH	s92j
St Gabriel's School	Boys & Girls, 0-18	Day	Newbury, RG20 9BD	s49b
St George's Ascot	*Girls, 11-18*	*Day & Boarding*	**Ascot, SL5 7DZ**	s47d
St George's School Windsor Castle	Boys & Girls, 3-13	Day & Boarding	Windsor, SL4 1QF	s51q
St John's Beaumont	Boys & Girls, 3-13	Day & Boarding	Old Windsor, SL4 2JN	s72j
St Joseph's College Reading	Boys & Girls, 3-18	Day	Reading, RG1 5JT	s65j
St Mary's School Ascot	Girls, 11-18	Day & Boarding	Ascot, SL5 9JF	s89j
St Piran's	Boys & Girls, 2-11	Day	Maidenhead, SL6 7LZ	s17l
Sunningdale School	Boys, 7-13	Day & Boarding	Sunningdale, SL5 9PY	s89p
The Abbey School	Girls, 3-18	Day	Reading, RG1 5DZ	t65d
The Marist School	Girls 2-18, Boys 2-4	Day	Sunninghill, SL5 7PS	t97p
Thorngrove School	Boys & Girls, 2-13	Day	Highclere, RG20 9PS	t29p
Upton House School	Boys & Girls, 2-11	Day	Windsor, SL4 3DF	u73d
Waverley School	Boys & Girls, 0-11	Day	Wokingham, RG40 4YD	w24y
Wellington College	*Boys & Girls, 13-18*	*Day & Boarding*	**Crowthorne, RG45 7PU**	w57p

Discover more about schools listed in the Schools' Directory by using the quick link code to jump to the page on our website, e.g. *attain.guide/w57p*

Buckinghamshire

attain guide?h25q

Akeley Wood	Boys & Girls, 1-18	Day	Buckingham, MK18 5AE	a55a
Ashfold School	Boys & Girls, 3-13	Day & Boarding	Aylesbury, HP18 9NG	a59n
Broughton Manor Prep School	Boys & Girls, 1-11	Day	Milton Keynes, MK10 9AA	b69a
Caldicott	Boys, 7-13	Day & Boarding	Slough, SL2 3SL	c83s
Chesham Prep School	Boys & Girls, 3-11	Day	Chesham, HP5 3QF	c23q
Dair House School	Boys & Girls, 3-11	Day	Farnham Royal, SL2 3BY	d43b
Davenies School	Boys, 4-13	Day	Beaconsfield, HP9 1AA	d51a
Gateway School	Boys & Girls, 2-11	Day	Great Missenden, HP16 9AA	g69a
Gayhurst School	Boys & Girls, 3-11	Day	Gerrards Cross, SL9 8RJ	g98r
Godstowe Preparatory School	Girls 3-13, Boys 3-7	Day & Boarding	High Wycombe, HP13 6PR	g76p
Heatherton School	**Girls 2-11, Boys 2-5**	**Day**	**Amersham, HP6 5QB**	h25q
High March School	Girls, 2-11	Day	Beaconsfield, HP9 2PZ	h22p
Maltman's Green	Girls, 2-11	Day	Gerrards Cross, SL9 8RR	m98r
Milton Keynes Prep School	Boys & Girls, 0-11	Day	Milton Keynes, MK3 7EG	m37e
Pipers Corner School	Girls, 4-18	Day	High Wycombe, HP15 6LP	p76l
St Mary's School, Gerrards Cross	Girls, 3-18	Day	Gerrards Cross, SL9 8JQ	s68j
Stowe School	Boys & Girls, 13-18	Day & Boarding	Buckingham, MK18 5EH	s75e
Swanbourne House	Boys & Girls, 3-13	Day & Boarding	Winslow, MK17 0HZ	s50h
The Beacon School	**Boys, 3-13**	**Day**	**Chesham Bois, HP6 5PF**	t75p
Thornton College	Girls 3-18	Day & Boarding	Milton Keynes, MK17 0HJ	t00h
Thorpe House School	Boys, 4-16	Day	Gerrards Cross, SL9 8QA	t68q
Wycombe Abbey	**Girls, 11-18**	**Day & Boarding**	**High Wycombe, HP11 1PE**	w21p

The Beacon School
Day · Boys, 3-13 · Chesham Bois, HP6 5PF

Wycombe Abbey
Day · Girls, 11-18 · High Wycombe, HP11 1PE

Schools' Directory

East Sussex

Bede's
Day · Boys & Girls, 0-18 · Upper Dicker, BN27 3QH

Brighton College
Day · Boys & Girls, 3-18 · Brighton, BN2 0AL

Battle Abbey School	Boys & Girls, 2-18	Day & Boarding	Battle, TN33 0AD	b80a
Bede's	Boys & Girls, 0-18	Day & Boarding	Upper Dicker, BN27 3QH	b73q
Brighton College	Boys & Girls, 3-18	Day & Boarding	Brighton, BN2 0AL	b40a
Brighton Girls	Girls, 3-18	Day	Brighton, BN1 3AT	b83a
Eastbourne College	Boys & Girls, 13-18	Day & Boarding	Eastbourne, BN21 4JX	e44j
Lancing College Prep Hove	Boys & Girls, 3-13	Day	Hove, BN3 6LU	l36l
Lewes Old Grammar School	Boys & Girls, 3-18	Day	Lewes, BN7 1XS	l81x
Mayfield School	Girls, 11-18	Day & Boarding	Mayfield, TN20 6PH	m36p
Roedean School	Girls, 11-18	Day & Boarding	Brighton, BN2 5RQ	r55r
Skippers Hill Manor Prep School	Boys & Girls, 3-13	Day	Mayfield, TN20 6HR	s26h
St Andrew's Prep	Boys & Girls, 1-13	Day & Boarding	Eastbourne, BN20 7RP	s47r
St Christopher's School	Boys & Girls, 4-13	Day	Hove, BN3 4AD	s14a
Vinehall School	Boys & Girls, 2-13	Day & Boarding	Robertsbridge, TN32 5JL	v05j

Eastbourne College
Day · Boys & Girls, 13-18 · Eastbourne, BN21 4JX

St Andrew's Prep
Day · Boys & Girls, 1-13 · Eastbourne, BN20 7RP

Hampshire

Ballard School	Boys & Girls, 2-16	Day	New Milton, BH25 5SU	b55s
Bedales School	Boys & Girls, 3-18	Day & Boarding	Petersfield, GU32 2DG	b52d
Boundary Oak School	Boys & Girls, 2-16	Day & Boarding	Fareham, PO17 5BL	b15b
Churcher's College	Boys & Girls, 3-18	Day	Petersfield, GU31 4AS	c54a
Durlston Prep & Senior School	Boys & Girls, 2-16	Day	New Milton, BH25 7AQ	d37a
Embley	Boys & Girls, 2-18	Day & Boarding	Romsey, SO51 6ZE	e86z
Farleigh School	Boys & Girls, 3-13	Day & Boarding	Andover, SP11 7PW	f07p
Farnborough Hill	Girls, 11-18	Day	Farnborough, GU14 8AT	f28a
Forres Sandle Manor	Boys & Girls, 2-16	Day & Boarding	Fordingbridge, SP6 1NS	f01n
Highfield and Brookham Schools	Boys & Girls, 2-13	Day & Boarding	Liphook, GU30 7LQ	h07l
King Edward VI Preparatory School	**Boys & Girls, 3-11**	**Day**	**Romsey, SO51 9ZH**	s99z
King Edward VI School	Boys & Girls, 11-18	Day	Southampton, SO15 5UQ	k85u
Lord Wandsworth College	Boys & Girls, 11-18	Day & Boarding	Hook, RG29 1TB	l21t
Pilgrims' School	Boys, 4-13	Day & Boarding	Winchester, SO23 9LT	p39l
Portsmouth High School	Girls, 3-18	Day	Southsea, PO5 3EQ	p33e
Prince's Mead School	Boys & Girls, 4-11	Day	Winchester, SO21 1AN	p51a
Ryde School	**Boys & Girls, 2-18**	**Day & Boarding**	**Ryde, PO33 3BE**	r73b
St Neot's Preparatory School	Boys & Girls, 2-13	Day	Basingstoke, RG27 0PN	s20p
St Nicholas' School	Girls 3-16, Boys 3-7	Day	Church Crookham, GU52 0RF	s40r
St Swithun's School	**Girls, 3-18**	**Day & Boarding**	**Winchester, SO21 1HA**	s71h
The Portsmouth Grammar School	Boys & Girls, 2-18	Day	Portsmouth, PO1 2LN	t62l
Twyford School	Boys & Girls, 2-13	Day	Winchester, SO21 1NW	t71n
Walhampton	Boys & Girls, 2-13	Day & Boarding	Lymington, SO41 5ZG	w75z
Wellesley Prep School	Boys & Girls, 2-13	Day	Basingstoke, RG27 0AR	d20a

King Edward VI Preparatory School
Day · Boys & Girls, 3-11 · Romsey, SO51 9ZH

Ryde School
Day · Boys & Girls, 2-18 · Ryde, PO33 3BE

Schools' Directory

West Hill Park	Boys & Girls, 2-13	Day & Boarding	Titchfield, PO14 4BS	w24b
Winchester College	Boys 13-18, Girls 16-18	Boarding	Winchester, SO23 9NA	w99n
Yateley Manor School	Boys & Girls, 2-16	Day	Yateley, GU46 7UQ	y57u

Kent

Ashford School	Boys & Girls, 0-18	Day & Boarding	Ashford, TN24 8PB	a08p
Babington House School	Boys & Girls, 3-18	Day	Chislehurst, BR7 5ES	b05e
Beechwood School	Boys & Girls, 3-18	Day & Boarding	Tunbridge Wells, TN2 3QD	b93q
Benenden School	Girls, 11-18	Day & Boarding	Cranbrook, TN17 4AA	b04a
Bethany School	Boys & Girls, 11-18	Day & Boarding	Cranbrook, TN17 1LB	b31l
Bickley Park School	Boys & Girls, 2-13	Day	Bromley, BR1 2DS	b22d
Cobham Hall School	Boys & Girls, 11-18	Day & Boarding	Cobham, DA12 3BL	c73b
Dover College	Boys & Girls, 3-18	Day & Boarding	Dover, CT17 9RH	d49r
Dulwich Cranbrook	Boys & Girls, 2-16	Day & Boarding	Cranbrook, TN17 3NP	d63n
Farringtons School	Boys & Girls, 3-18	Day & Boarding	Chislehurst, BR7 6LR	f06l
Granville School	Girls 3-11, Boys 3-4	Day	Sevenoaks, TN13 3LJ	g63l
Hilden Grange School	Boys & Girls, 3-13	Day	Tonbridge, TN10 3BX	h83b
Hilden Oaks School & Nursery	Boys & Girls, 1-11	Day	Tonbridge, TN10 3BU	h73b
Holmewood House	Boys & Girls, 3-13	Day & Boarding	Tunbridge Wells, TN3 0EB	h40e
Kent College	**Boys & Girls, 0-18**	**Day & Boarding**	**Canterbury, CT2 9DT**	k19d
Kent College Pembury	Girls 3-18, Boys 3-11	Day & Boarding	Pembury, TN2 4AX	k34a
King's Rochester	Boys & Girls, 3-18	Day & Boarding	Rochester, ME1 1TE	k91t
King's School Canterbury	Boys & Girls, 3-18	Day & Boarding	Canterbury, CT1 2ES	k82e
Lorenden Preparatory School	Boys & Girls, 3-11	Day	Faversham, ME13 0EN	l40e
Marlborough House School	Boys & Girls, 3-13	Day & Boarding	Hawkhurst, TN18 4PY	m74p
Northbourne Park School	Boys & Girls, 2-13	Day & Boarding	Deal, CT14 0NW	n40n
Radnor House School Sevenoaks	Boys & Girls, 2-18	Day	Sevenoaks, TN14 6AE	r76a
Rose Hill School	Boys & Girls, 3-13	Day	Tunbridge Wells, TN4 9SY	r59s
Russell House School	Boys & Girls, 2-11	Day	Otford, TN14 5QU	r95q
Sackville School	Boys & Girls, 11-18	Day	Tonbridge, TN11 9HN	s89h
Saint Ronan's	Boys & Girls, 3-13	Day & Boarding	Hawkhurst, TN18 5DJ	s35d
Sevenoaks Preparatory School	Boys & Girls, 2-13	Day	Sevenoaks, TN15 0JU	s80j
Sevenoaks School	Boys & Girls, 11-18	Day & Boarding	Sevenoaks, TN13 1HU	s91h
Solefield School	Boys & Girls, 3-13	Day	Sevenoaks, TN13 1PH	s91p
Somerhill	Boys & Girls, 2-13	Day	Tonbridge, TN11 0NJ	s60n

Attain Guide 2025

Kent College
Day · Boys & Girls, 0-18 · Canterbury, CT2 9DT k19d

Tonbridge School
Day · Boys, 13-18 · Tonbridge, TN9 1JP t51j

Spring Grove	Boys & Girls, 2-11	Day	Wye, TN25 5EZ	s55e
St Edmund's School Canterbury	Boys & Girls, 3-18	Day & Boarding	Canterbury, CT2 8HU	s48h
St Lawrence College	**Boys & Girls, 3-18**	**Day & Boarding**	**Ramsgate, CT11 7AE**	s27a
St Michael's Prep School	Boys & Girls, 2-13	Day	Sevenoaks, TN14 5RY	s15r
Sutton Valence School	Boys & Girls, 2-18	Day & Boarding	Maidstone, ME17 3HL	s53h
The New Beacon	Boys, 4-13	Day & Boarding	Sevenoaks, TN13 2PB	n62p
Tonbridge School	**Boys, 13-18**	**Day & Boarding**	**Tonbridge, TN9 1JP**	t51j
Walthamstow Hall	Girls, 2-18	Day	Sevenoaks, TN13 3UL	w43u

Oxfordshire

attain.guide/s54b

Abingdon Preparatory School	Boys & Girls, 4-13	Day	Frilford, OX13 5NX	a05n
Abingdon School	Boys & Girls, 11-18	Day & Boarding	Abingdon, OX14 1DE	a61d
Bloxham School	Boys & Girls, 11-18	Day & Boarding	Banbury, OX15 4PE	b74p
Bruern Abbey School	Boys, 8-16	Day & Boarding	Chesterton, OX26 1UY	b21u
Carrdus School	Boys & Girls, 3-11	Day	Banbury, OX17 2BS	c32b
Chandlings	Boys & Girls, 2-11	Day	Oxford, OX1 5ND	c85n
Christ Church Cathedral School	Boys 3-13, Girls 3-7	Day & Boarding	Oxford, OX1 1QW	c11q
Cokethorpe School	Boys & Girls, 4-18	Day	Witney, OX29 7PU	c27p
Cothill House School	Boys & Girls, 8-13	Day & Boarding	Abingdon, OX13 6JL	c16j
Cranford House School	Boys & Girls, 3-18	Day	Wallingford, OX10 9HT	c79h
d'Overbroeck's Oxford	Boys & Girls, 11-18	Day & Boarding	Oxford, OX2 6HZ	d06h
Dragon School, Oxford	Boys & Girls, 4-13	Day & Boarding	Oxford, OX2 6SS	d96s
Headington School	Girls 3-18, Boys 3-11	Day & Boarding	Oxford, OX3 7TD	h47t
Kingham Hill School	Boys & Girls, 11-18	Day & Boarding	Chipping Norton, OX7 6TH	k06t
Magdalen College School	Boys 7-18, Girls 16-18	Day	Oxford, OX4 1DZ	m51d

Schools' Directory

| Moulsford Preparatory School | Boys & Girls, 3-13 | Day & Boarding | Wallingford, OX10 9HR | m79h |
Moulsford Preparatory School	Boys & Girls, 3-13	Day & Boarding	Wallingford, OX10 9HR	m79h
New College School	Boys, 4-13	Day	Oxford, OX1 3UA	n63u
Our Lady's Abingdon	Boys & Girls, 7-18	Day	Abingdon, OX14 3PS	o83p
Oxford High School	Girls, 4-18	Day	Oxford, OX2 6XA	o66x
Radley College	Boys, 13-18	Boarding	Abingdon, OX14 2HR	r12h
Rupert House School	Boys & Girls, 3-11	Day	Henley-on-Thames, RG9 2BN	r92b
Shiplake College	**Boys & Girls, 11-18**	**Day & Boarding**	**Henley-on-Thames, RG9 4BW**	s54b
Sibford School	Boys & Girls, 3-18	Day & Boarding	Banbury, OX15 5QL	s45q
St Edward's School, Oxford	Boys & Girls, 13-18	Day & Boarding	Oxford, OX2 7NN	s17n
St Helen & St Katharine	Girls, 9-18	Day	Abingdon, OX14 1BE	s41b
St Hugh's School	Boys & Girls, 3-13	Day & Boarding	Faringdon, SN7 8PT	s08p
St Mary's School	Boys & Girls, 3-11	Day	Henley-on-Thames, RG9 1HS	s01h
Summer Fields	Boys, 4-13	Day & Boarding	Oxford, OX2 7EN	s27e
The Manor Preparatory School	Boys & Girls, 2-11	Day	Abingdon, OX13 6LN	m06l
The Oratory Prep School	**Boys & Girls, 2-13**	**Day & Boarding**	**Reading, RG8 7SF**	o87s
The Oratory School	**Boys & Girls, 11-18**	**Day & Boarding**	**Reading, RG8 0PJ**	t70p
Tudor Hall School	Girls, 11-18	Day & Boarding	Banbury, OX16 9UR	t89u
Wychwood School	Boys & Girls, 11-18	Day & Boarding	Oxford, OX2 6JR	w86j

s54b — Oxfordshire

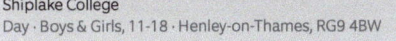

Shiplake College
Day · Boys & Girls, 11-18 · Henley-on-Thames, RG9 4BW

t70p — Oxfordshire

The Oratory School
Day · Boys & Girls, 11-18 · Reading, RG8 0PJ

Surrey

Aberdour School	Boys & Girls, 2-13	Day	Burgh Heath, KT20 6AJ	a46a
Aldro School	Boys & Girls, 7-13	Day & Boarding	Godalming, GU8 6AS	a06a
Amesbury	Boys & Girls, 2-13	Day	Hindhead, GU26 6BL	a26b
Banstead Preparatory School	Boys & Girls, 2-11	Day	Banstead, SM7 3RA	b53r
Barfield School	Boys & Girls, 2-11	Day	Farnham, GU10 1PB	b91p

Attain Guide 2025

Cranleigh School
Day · Boys & Girls, 7-18 · Cranleigh, GU6 8QQ

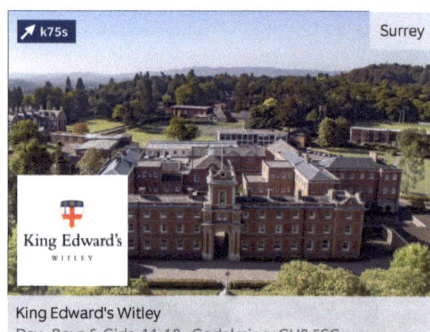

King Edward's Witley
Day · Boys & Girls, 11-18 · Godalming, GU8 5SG

Barrow Hills School	*Boys & Girls, 2-13*	*Day*	**Godalming, GU8 5NY**	b95n
Bishopsgate School	*Boys & Girls, 3-13*	*Day*	Egham, TW20 0YJ	b90y
Box Hill School	*Boys & Girls, 11-18*	*Day & Boarding*	Dorking, RH5 6EA	b16e
Caterham School	*Boys & Girls, 3-18*	*Day & Boarding*	Caterham, CR3 6YA	c96y
Charterhouse	*Boys & Girls, 13-18*	*Day & Boarding*	Godalming, GU7 2DX	c72d
Chinthurst School	*Boys & Girls, 2-11*	*Day*	Tadworth, KT20 5QZ	c65q
City of London Freemen's School	*Boys & Girls, 7-18*	*Day & Boarding*	Ashstead Park, KT21 1ET	c61e
Claremont Fan Court School	*Boys & Girls, 2-18*	*Day*	Esher, KT10 9LY	c89l
Collingwood School	*Boys & Girls, 3-11*	*Day*	Wallington, SM6 0BD	c60b
Coworth Flexlands School	*Boys & Girls, 2-11*	*Day*	Chobham, GU24 8TE	c78t
Cranleigh School	*Boys & Girls, 7-18*	*Day & Boarding*	**Cranleigh, GU6 8QQ**	c58q
Cranmore School	*Boys 2-16, Girls 2-7*	*Day*	West Horsley, KT24 6AT	c16a
Cumnor House School	*Boys & Girls, 2-13*	*Day*	South Croydon, CR2 6DA	c86d
Danes Hill School	*Boys & Girls, 3-13*	*Day*	Oxshott, KT22 0JG	d70j
Downsend School	*Boys & Girls, 2-16*	*Day*	Leatherhead, KT22 8TJ	d58t
Duke of Kent School	*Boys & Girls, 3-16*	*Day*	Ewhurst, GU6 7NS	d47n
Dunottar School	*Boys & Girls, 11-18*	*Day*	Reigate, RH2 7EL	d47e
Edgeborough	*Boys & Girls, 2-13*	*Day & Boarding*	Farnham, GU10 3AH	e73a
Epsom College	*Boys & Girls, 11-18*	*Day & Boarding*	Epsom, KT17 4JQ	e64j
Ewell Castle School	*Boys & Girls, 2-18*	*Day*	Ewell, KT17 2AW	e32a
Feltonfleet School	*Boys & Girls, 3-13*	*Day & Boarding*	Cobham, KT11 1DR	f11d
Frensham Heights	*Boys & Girls, 3-18*	*Day & Boarding*	Farnham, GU10 4EA	f44e
Glenesk School	*Boys & Girls, 2-7*	*Day*	East Horsley, KT24 6NS	g56n
Greenfield School	*Boys & Girls, 3-11*	*Day*	Woking, GU22 7TP	g77t
Guildford High School	*Girls, 4-18*	*Day*	Guildford, GU1 1SJ	g21s

Schools' Directory

Hall Grove	Boys & Girls, 3-13	Day & Boarding	Bagshot, GU19 5HZ	h65h
Halstead St Andrew's	Boys & Girls, 2-16	Day	Woking, GU21 4EE	h34e
Hazelwood School	Boys & Girls, 1-13	Day	Oxted, RH8 0QU	h20q
Hoe Bridge School	Boys & Girls, 2-16	Day	Woking, GU22 8JE	h58j
Holy Cross Preparatory School	Girls, 3-11	Day	Kingston upon Thames, KT2 7NU	h87n
Homefield Preparatory School	Boys, 4-13	Day	Sutton, SM1 2TE	h62t
Hurtwood House	Boys & Girls, 15-19	Day & Boarding	Dorking, RH5 6NU	h06n
King Edward's Witley	**Boys & Girls, 11-18**	**Day & Boarding**	**Godalming, GU8 5SG**	k75s
Kingston Grammar School	Boys & Girls, 11-18	Day	Kingston upon Thames, KT2 6PY	k66p
Kingswood House School	Boys & Girls, 4-16	Day	Epsom, KT19 8LG	k28l
Lingfield College	**Boys & Girls, 0-18**	**Day**	**Lingfield, RH7 6PN**	l16p
Longacre School	Boys & Girls, 2-11	Day	Guildford, GU5 0NQ	l70n
Manor House School	Girls, 2-16	Day	Leatherhead, KT23 4EN	m64e
Marymount London	Girls, 11-18	Day & Boarding	Kingston upon Thames, KT2 7PE	m47p
Micklefield School	Boys & Girls, 3-11	Day	Reigate, RH2 9DU	m89d
Milbourne Lodge School	Boys & Girls, 4-13	Day	Esher, KT10 9EG	m39e
Notre Dame School	Girls 2-18, Boys 2-4	Day	Cobham, KT11 1HA	n41h
Oakwood School, Purley	Boys & Girls, 4-11	Day	Purley, CR8 2AN	o52a
Parkside School	Boys, 2-13	Day	Stoke D'abernon, KT11 3PX	p63p
Prior's Field	Girls, 11-18	Day & Boarding	Godalming, GU7 2RH	p12r
Reed's School	**Boys 11-18, Girls 16-18**	**Day & Boarding**	**Cobham, KT11 2ES**	r22e
Reigate Grammar School	Boys & Girls, 11-18	Day	Reigate, RH2 0QS	r50q
Reigate St. Mary's Prep School	Boys & Girls, 2-11	Day	Reigate, RH2 7RN	r87r
RGS Prep	Boys, 3-11	Day	Guildford, GU1 2EL	r32e
Ripley Court School	Boys & Girls, 3-11	Day	Ripley, GU23 6NE	r66n

l16p — Surrey
Lingfield College
Day · Boys & Girls, 0-18 · Lingfield, RH7 6PN

r22e — Surrey
Reed's School
Day · Boys 11-18, Girls 16-18 · Cobham, KT11 2ES

Attain Guide 2025

School	Pupils	Type	Location	Ref
Rokeby School	Boys, 4-13	Day	Kingston upon Thames, KT2 7PB	r17p
Rowan Preparatory School	Girls, 2-11	Day	Esher, KT10 0LX	r60l
Royal Grammar School Guildford	Boys, 11-18	Day	Guildford, GU1 3BB	r83b
Royal Russell School	Boys & Girls, 3-18	Day & Boarding	Croydon, CR9 5BX	r05b
Rydes Hill Prep School & Nursery	Girls 3-11, Boys 3-7	Day	Guildford, GU2 8BP	r28b
Shrewsbury House & The Rowans	Boys 2-13, Girls 2-7	Day	Surbiton, KT6 6RL	s16r
Sir William Perkins's School	Boys & Girls, 11-18	Day	Chertsey, KT16 9BN	s29b
St Catherine's School	Girls, 3-18	Day & Boarding	Guildford, GU5 0DF	s00d
St Edmund's School	Boys & Girls, 2-16	Day & Boarding	Hindhead, GU26 6BH	s76b
St George's Weybridge	Boys & Girls, 3-18	Day	Weybridge, KT15 2QS	s82q
St Hilary's Preparatory School	Boys & Girls, 2-11	Day	Godalming, GU7 1RZ	s31r
St Ives School	Boys & Girls, 2-11	Day	Haslemere, GU27 2ES	s32e
St James Senior Boys' School	Boys, 11-18	Day	Ashford, TW15 3DZ	s13d
St John's Leatherhead	Boys & Girls, 11-18	Day & Boarding	Leatherhead, KT22 8SP	s18s
St Teresa's Effingham	Girls, 2-18	Day & Boarding	Dorking, RH5 6ST	s56s
Surbiton High School	Girls 4-18, Boys 4-11	Day	Kingston upon Thames, KT1 2JT	s62j
The Hawthorns School	Boys & Girls, 1-13	Day	Bletchingley, RH1 4QJ	t84q
The Royal School, Surrey	Boys & Girls, 0-18	Day & Boarding	Haslemere, GU27 1HQ	t41h
Tormead School	Girls, 4-18	Day	Guildford, GU1 2JD	t82j
Trinity School	Boys 11-18, Girls 16-18	Day	Croydon, CR9 7AT	t07a
Woldingham School	**Girls, 11-18**	**Day & Boarding**	**Woldingham, CR3 7YA**	w67y
Woodcote House	Boys, 7-13	Day & Boarding	Windlesham, GU20 6PF	w36p
Yehudi Menuhin School	Boys & Girls, 7-18	Day & Boarding	Cobham, KT11 3QQ	y93q

Woldingham School
Day · Girls, 11-18 · Woldingham, CR3 7YA

Lancing College
Day · Boys & Girls, 13-18 · Lancing, BN15 0RW

Schools' Directory

West Sussex

attain.guide/l10r

Ardingly College	Boys & Girls, 2-18	Day & Boarding	Haywards Heath, RH17 6SQ	a26s
Brambletye School	Boys & Girls, 2-13	Day & Boarding	East Grinstead, RH19 3PD	b53p
Burgess Hill Girls	Girls 2-18, Boys 2-4	Day & Boarding	Burgess Hill, RH15 0EG	b20e
Christ's Hospital	Boys & Girls, 11-18	Day & Boarding	Horsham, RH13 0YP	c00y
Copthorne Prep School	Boys & Girls, 2-13	Day & Boarding	Copthorne, RH10 3HR	c13h
Cottesmore School	Boys & Girls, 4-13	Day & Boarding	Crawley, RH11 9AU	c49a
Cumnor House Sussex	Boys & Girls, 4-13	Day & Boarding	Haywards Heath, RH17 7HT	c87h
Dorset House Prep School	Boys & Girls, 4-13	Day & Boarding	Pulborough, RH20 1PB	d91p
Farlington School	Boys & Girls, 0-18	Day & Boarding	Horsham, RH12 3PN	f53p
Great Ballard	Boys & Girls, 2-16	Day & Boarding	Chichester, PO18 0LR	g60l
Great Walstead School	Boys & Girls, 2-13	Day & Boarding	Haywards Heath, RH16 2QL	g72q
Handcross Park School	Boys & Girls, 2-13	Day & Boarding	Haywards Heath, RH17 6HF	h36h
Hurstpierpoint College	Boys & Girls, 3-18	Day & Boarding	Hurstpierpoint, BN6 9JS	h89j
Lancing College	**Boys & Girls, 13-18**	**Day & Boarding**	**Lancing, BN15 0RW**	**l10r**
Lancing College Prep Worthing	**Boys & Girls, 2-13**	**Day**	**Worthing, BN14 8HU**	**l38h**
Oakwood School, Chichester	Boys & Girls, 2-11	Day	Chichester, PO18 9AN	o09a
Our Lady of Sion School	Boys & Girls, 3-18	Day	Worthing, BN11 4BL	o44b
Pennthorpe School	Boys & Girls, 2-13	Day	Rudgwick, RH12 3HJ	p73h
Prebendal School	Boys & Girls, 3-13	Day & Boarding	Chichester, PO19 1LX	p31l
Seaford College	Boys & Girls, 7-18	Day & Boarding	Petworth, GU28 0NB	s90n
Sompting Abbotts Prep School	Boys & Girls, 2-13	Day	Sompting, BN15 0AZ	s50a
Westbourne House School	Boys & Girls, 3-13	Day & Boarding	Chichester, PO20 2BH	w12b
Windlesham House School	Boys & Girls, 4-13	Day & Boarding	Pulborough, RH20 4AY	w44a
Worth School	Boys & Girls, 11-18	Day & Boarding	Turners Hill, RH10 4SD	w24s

Discover more about schools listed in the Schools' Directory by using the quick link code to jump to the page on our website, e.g. *attain.guide/l10r*

Attain Guide 2025

South West

Use the QR code to learn more about schools in the South West

Bristol

↗ attain.guide/b13b

Badminton School	Girls, 4-18	Day & Boarding	Westbury-on-Trym, BS9 3BA	↗ b13b
Bristol Grammar School	Boys & Girls, 4-18	Day	Bristol, BS8 1SR	↗ b51s
Clifton College	Boys & Girls, 3-18	Day & Boarding	Clifton, BS8 3JH	↗ c73j
Clifton High School	Boys & Girls, 3-18	Day & Boarding	Clifton, BS8 3JD	↗ c93j
Collegiate School	Boys & Girls, 3-18	Day	Stapleton, BS16 1BJ	↗ c91b
Queen Elizabeth's Hospital	Boys 7-18, Girls 16-18	Day	Clifton, BS8 1JX	↗ q21j
Redmaids' High School	Girls, 7-18	Day	Bristol, BS9 3AW	↗ r53a
The Downs School	Boys & Girls, 4-13	Day	Wraxall, BS48 1PF	↗ t01p

Badminton School
Day · Girls, 4-18 · Westbury-on-Trym, BS9 3BA

The King's School Gloucester
Day · Boys & Girls, 3-18 · Gloucester, GL1 2BG

Cornwall

Polwhele House School	Boys & Girls, 3-13	Day & Boarding	Truro, TR4 9AE	↗ p49a
Truro High School for Girls	Girls, 4-18	Day & Boarding	Truro, TR1 2HU	↗ t42h
Truro School	Boys & Girls, 3-18	Day & Boarding	Truro, TR1 1TH	↗ t51t

Devon

Abbey School	Boys & Girls, 0-11	Day	Torquay, TQ1 4PR	↗ a04p
Blundell's School	Boys & Girls, 3-18	Day & Boarding	Tiverton, EX16 4DN	↗ b74d
Exeter Cathedral School	Boys & Girls, 3-13	Day & Boarding	Exeter, EX1 1HX	↗ e41h
Exeter School	Boys & Girls, 3-18	Day	Exeter, EX2 4NS	↗ e04n
Mount Kelly College	Boys & Girls, 2-18	Day & Boarding	Tavistock, PL19 0HZ	↗ m40h
Plymouth College	Boys & Girls, 3-18	Day & Boarding	Plymouth, PL4 6RN	↗ p96r

Schools' Directory

Shebbear College	*Boys & Girls, 4-18*	Day & Boarding	Shebbear, EX21 5HJ	s25h
St John's School, Sidmouth	*Boys & Girls, 2-16*	Day & Boarding	Sidmouth, EX10 8RG	s78r
St Peter's Preparatory School	*Boys & Girls, 3-13*	Day & Boarding	Lympstone, EX8 5AU	s35a
Stover School	*Boys & Girls, 3-18*	Day & Boarding	Newton Abbot, TQ12 6QG	s66q
The Maynard School	*Girls, 4-18*	Day	Exeter, EX1 1SJ	t61s
Trinity School Teignmouth	*Boys & Girls, 2-18*	Day & Boarding	Teignmouth, TQ14 8LY	t68l
West Buckland School	*Boys & Girls, 3-18*	Day & Boarding	Barnstaple, EX32 0SX	w70s

Dorset

Bournemouth Collegiate School	***Boys & Girls, 3-18***	**Day & Boarding**	**Bournemouth, BH5 2DY**	**b42d**
Bryanston School	*Boys & Girls, 3-18*	Day & Boarding	Blandford Forum, DT11 0PX	b00p
Canford School	*Boys & Girls, 13-18*	Day & Boarding	Wimborne, BH21 3AD	c63a
Castle Court School	*Boys & Girls, 2-13*	Day	Wimborne, BH21 3RF	c13r
Clayesmore School	*Boys & Girls, 8-18*	Day & Boarding	Blandford Forum, DT11 8LL	c08l
Dumpton School	*Boys & Girls, 2-13*	Day	Wimborne, BH21 7AF	d77a
Hanford School	*Girls, 7-13*	Day & Boarding	Blandford, DT11 8HL	h68h
Leweston School	*Boys & Girls, 0-18*	Day & Boarding	Sherborne, DT9 6EN	l56e
Milton Abbey School	*Boys & Girls, 13-18*	Day & Boarding	Blandford Forum, DT11 0BZ	m30b
Port Regis	*Boys & Girls, 3-13*	Day & Boarding	Shaftesbury, SP7 9QA	p89q
Sherborne Girls	*Girls, 11-18*	Day & Boarding	Sherborne, DT9 3QN	s73q
Sherborne Preparatory School	*Boys & Girls, 3-13*	Day & Boarding	Sherborne, DT9 3NY	s33n
Sherborne School	*Boys, 13-18*	Day & Boarding	Sherborne, DT9 3AP	s23a
Sunninghill Preparatory School	*Boys & Girls, 0-13*	Day	Dorchester, DT1 1EB	s21e
Talbot Heath School	***Girls, 3-18***	**Day & Boarding**	**Bournemouth, BH4 9NJ**	**t79n**
Yarrells Preparatory School	*Boys & Girls, 2-13*	Day	Upton, BH16 5EU	y85e

b42d — Dorset
Bournemouth Collegiate School
Day · Boys & Girls, 3-18 · Bournemouth, BH5 2DY

t79n — Dorset
Talbot Heath School
Day · Girls, 3-18 · Bournemouth, BH4 9NJ

Gloucestershire

Beaudesert Park School	Boys & Girls, 4-13	Day & Boarding	Stroud, GL6 9AF	b19a
Berkhampstead School	Boys & Girls, 0-11	Day	Cheltenham, GL52 2QA	b12q
Bredon School	Boys & Girls, 3-18	Day & Boarding	Tewkesbury, GL20 6AH	b36a
Cheltenham College	Boys & Girls, 3-18	Day & Boarding	Cheltenham, GL53 7LD	c37l
Cheltenham Ladies' College	Girls, 11-18	Day & Boarding	Cheltenham, GL50 3EP	c33e
Dean Close School	Boys & Girls, 3-18	Day & Boarding	Cheltenham, GL51 6HE	d46h
Hatherop Castle Prep School	Boys & Girls, 2-13	Day & Boarding	Cirencester, GL7 3NB	h23n
Kitebrook Preparatory School	Boys & Girls, 3-13	Day & Boarding	Moreton-in-Marsh, GL56 0RP	k70r
Rendcomb College	Boys & Girls, 3-18	Day & Boarding	Cirencester, GL7 7HA	r07h
St Edward's School, Cheltenham	Boys & Girls, 1-18	Day	Cheltenham, GL53 8EY	s28e
The King's School Gloucester	**Boys & Girls, 3-18**	**Day**	**Gloucester, GL1 2BG**	k02b
The Richard Pate School	Boys & Girls, 3-11	Day	Cheltenham, GL53 9RP	r79r
Tockington Manor School	Boys & Girls, 2-13	Day & Boarding	Bristol, BS32 4NY	t34n
Westonbirt School	Boys & Girls, 2-18	Day & Boarding	Tetbury, GL8 8QG	w88q
Wycliffe College	Boys & Girls, 2-18	Day & Boarding	Stonehouse, GL20 2JQ	w12j

Hazlegrove
Day · Boys & Girls, 2-13 · Yeovil, BA22 7JA

Dauntsey's School
Day · Boys & Girls, 11-18 · Devizes, SN10 4HE

Somerset

All Hallows School	Boys & Girls, 3-13	Day & Boarding	Shepton Mallet, BA4 4SF	a74s
Chard School	Boys & Girls, 0-11	Day	Chard, TA20 1QA	c91q
Downside School	Boys & Girls, 11-18	Day & Boarding	Bath, BA3 4RJ	d24r
Hazlegrove	**Boys & Girls, 2-13**	**Day & Boarding**	**Yeovil, BA22 7JA**	h37j
King Edward's School Bath	Boys & Girls, 3-18	Day	Bath, BA2 6HU	k26h
King's College Taunton	Boys & Girls, 2-18	Day & Boarding	Taunton, TA1 3LA	k93l
King's School Bruton	Boys & Girls, 13-18	Day & Boarding	Somerset, BA10 0ED	k30e

Schools' Directory

Kingswood School	Boys & Girls, 1-18	Day & Boarding	Bath, BA1 5RG	↗ k85r
Millfield School	Boys & Girls, 2-18	Day & Boarding	Street, BA16 0YD	↗ m10y
Monkton School	Boys & Girls, 2-18	Day & Boarding	Monkton Combe, BA2 7HG	↗ m47h
Perrott Hill	Boys & Girls, 3-13	Day & Boarding	Crewkerne, TA18 7SL	↗ p27s
Prior Park College	Boys & Girls, 11-18	Day & Boarding	Bath, BA2 5AH	↗ p45a
Queen's College Taunton	Boys & Girls, 0-18	Day & Boarding	Taunton, TA1 4QS	↗ q34q
Royal High School Bath GDST	Girls, 3-18	Day & Boarding	Bath, BA1 5SZ	↗ r25s
Sidcot School	Boys & Girls, 3-18	Day & Boarding	North Somerset, BS25 1PD	↗ s01p
Taunton School	Boys & Girls, 0-18	Day & Boarding	Taunton, TA2 6AD	↗ t26a
The Paragon School	Boys & Girls, 3-11	Day	Bath, BA2 4LT	↗ p44l
Wellington School	Boys & Girls, 3-18	Day & Boarding	Wellington, TA21 8NT	↗ w28n
Wells Cathedral School	Boys & Girls, 3-18	Day & Boarding	Wells, BA5 2ST	↗ w62s

Wiltshire

Chafyn Grove School	Boys & Girls, 3-16	Day & Boarding	Salisbury, SP1 1LR	↗ c21l
Cricklade Manor Preparatory	Boys & Girls, 2-13	Day & Boarding	Cricklade, SN6 6BB	↗ c56b
Dauntsey's School	**Boys & Girls, 11-18**	**Day & Boarding**	**Devizes, SN10 4HE**	↗ d14h
Godolphin School	Boys & Girls, 3-18	Day & Boarding	Salisbury, SP1 2RA	↗ g42r
Leehurst Swan	Boys & Girls, 4-16	Day	Salisbury, SP1 3BQ	↗ l53b
Marlborough College	**Boys & Girls, 13-18**	**Day & Boarding**	**Marlborough, SN8 1PA**	↗ m61p
Pinewood School	Boys & Girls, 3-13	Day & Boarding	Swindon, SN6 8HZ	↗ p38h
Salisbury Cathedral School	Boys & Girls, 3-13	Day & Boarding	Salisbury, SP1 2EQ	↗ s62e
Sandroyd School	**Boys & Girls, 2-11**	**Day & Boarding**	**Salisbury, SP5 5QD**	↗ s65q
St Francis School	Boys & Girls, 0-13	Day	Pewsey, SN9 5NT	↗ s75n
St Margaret's Preparatory School	**Boys & Girls, 2-11**	**Day**	**Calne, SN11 0DF**	↗ s30d

Marlborough College
Day · Boys & Girls, 13-18 · Marlborough, SN8 1PA

Sandroyd School
Day · Boys & Girls, 2-11 · Salisbury, SP5 5QD

St Mary's Calne	Girls, 11-18	Day & Boarding	Calne, SN11 0DF	↗ s10d
Stonar School	Boys & Girls, 2-18	Day & Boarding	Melksham, SN12 8NT	↗ s28n
Warminster School	Boys & Girls, 2-18	Day & Boarding	Warminster, BA12 8PJ	↗ w48p

St Margaret's Preparatory School
Day · Boys & Girls, 2-11 · Calne, SN11 0DF

St Mary's Calne
Day · Girls, 11-18 · Calne, SN11 0DF

East of England

Use the QR code to learn more about schools in the East of England

Bedfordshire

Bedford Girls' School	Girls, 7-18	Day	Bedford, MK42 0BX	↗ b70b
Bedford Modern School	Boys & Girls, 7-18	Day	Bedford, MK41 7NT	↗ b67n
Bedford School	Boys, 7-18	Day & Boarding	Bedford, MK40 2TU	↗ b62t
Orchard School and Nursery	Boys & Girls, 0-9	Day	Barton Le Clay, MK45 4LT	↗ o24l
Pilgrims Pre-Preparatory	Boys & Girls, 0-7	Day	Bedford, MK41 7QZ	↗ p57q

Cambridgeshire

Kimbolton School
Day · Boys & Girls, 4-18 · Huntingdon, PE28 0EA

St Faith's School
Day · Boys & Girls, 4-13 · Cambridge, CB2 8AG

Schools' Directory

Kimbolton School	Boys & Girls, 4-18	Day & Boarding	Huntingdon, PE28 0EA	k40e
King's College School	Boys & Girls, 4-13	Day & Boarding	Cambridge, CB3 9DN	k09d
King's Ely	Boys & Girls, 2-18	Day & Boarding	Ely, CB7 4EW	k74e
St Faith's School	Boys & Girls, 4-13	Day	Cambridge, CB2 8AG	s48a
St John's College School	Boys & Girls, 4-13	Day & Boarding	Cambridge, CB3 9AB	s19a
St Mary's School, Cambridge	Girls, 3-18	Day & Boarding	Cambridge, CB2 1LY	s21l
Stephen Perse Foundation	Boys & Girls, 1-18	Day	Cambridge, CB2 1HF	s21h
The Leys School	Boys & Girls, 11-18	Day & Boarding	Cambridge, CB2 7AD	t57a
The Perse School	Boys & Girls, 3-18	Day	Cambridge, CB2 2QF	t52q
The Peterborough School	Boys & Girls, 0-18	Day	Peterborough, PE3 6AP	t76a
Wisbech Grammar School	Boys & Girls, 3-18	Day	Wisbech, PE13 1RH	w21r

St Mary's School, Cambridge
Day · Girls, 3-18 · Cambridge, CB2 1LY

The Leys School
Day · Boys & Girls, 11-18 · Cambridge, CB2 7AD

Essex

Alleyn Court Preparatory School	Boys & Girls, 2-11	Day	Southend-on-Sea, SS3 0PW	a70p
Bancroft's School	Boys & Girls, 7-18	Day	Woodford Green, IG8 0RF	b30r
Brentwood School	Boys & Girls, 3-18	Day & Boarding	Brentwood, CM15 8EE	b28e
Chigwell School	Boys & Girls, 4-18	Day & Boarding	Chigwell, IG7 6QF	c66q
Elm Green Preparatory School	Boys & Girls, 4-11	Day	Chelmsford, CM3 4SU	e94s
Felsted School	Boys & Girls, 4-18	Day & Boarding	Felsted, CM6 3LL	f93l
Holmwood House School	Boys & Girls, 0-16	Day & Boarding	Colchester, CO3 9ST	h49s
Littlegarth School	Boys & Girls, 2-11	Day	Colchester, CO6 4JR	l74j
Loyola Preparatory School	Boys, 3-11	Day	Buckhurst Hill, IG9 5NH	l05n
Maldon Court Preparatory School	Boys & Girls, 3-11	Day	Maldon, CM9 4QE	m94q
New Hall School	Boys & Girls, 1-18	Day & Boarding	Boreham, CM3 3HS	n23h
St Aubyn's School	Boys & Girls, 3-11	Day	Woodford Green, IG8 9DU	s19d

Attain Guide 2025

Brentwood School
Day · Boys & Girls, 3-18 · Brentwood, CM15 8EE

Chigwell School
Day · Boys & Girls, 4-18 · Chigwell, IG7 6QF

St Cedd's School	Boys & Girls, 3-11	Day	Chelmsford, CM2 0AR	s10a
St Mary's, Colchester	Girls, 3-16	Day	Colchester, CO3 3RB	s53r
St Michael's Preparatory School	Boys & Girls, 3-11	Day	Leigh on Sea, SS9 2LP	s02l
The Ursuline Prep School Ilford	Boys & Girls, 3-11	Day	Ilford, IG1 4QR	u44q
Widford Lodge Preparatory School	Boys & Girls, 2-11	Day	Chelmsford, CM2 9AN	w59a
Woodford Green Prep School	**Boys & Girls, 3-11**	**Day**	**Woodford Green, IG8 0BZ**	**w80b**

Hertfordshire

Beechwood Park
Day · Boys & Girls, 3-13 · Markyate, near St Albans, AL3 8AW

Bishop's Stortford College
Day · Boys & Girls, 4-18 · Bishop's Stortford, CM23 2PQ

Abbot's Hill School	Girls 0-16, Boys 0-4	Day	Hemel Hempstead, HP3 8RP	a18r
Aldenham School	Boys & Girls, 3-18	Day & Boarding	Elstree, WD6 3AJ	a43a
Aldwickbury School	**Boys, 4-13**	**Day & Boarding**	**Harpenden, AL4 1AD**	**a81a**
Beechwood Park	**Boys & Girls, 3-13**	**Day & Boarding**	**Markyate, St Albans, AL3 8AW**	**b18a**
Berkhamsted School	**Boys & Girls, 0-18**	**Day & Boarding**	**Berkhamsted, HP4 2DJ**	**b12d**
Bishop's Stortford College	**Boys & Girls, 4-18**	**Day & Boarding**	**Bishop's Stortford, CM23 2PQ**	**b82p**
Charlotte House Prep School	Girls, 3-11	Day	Rickmansworth, WD3 4DU	c74d

Schools' Directory

School	Type	Day/Boarding	Location	Ref
Duncombe School	Boys & Girls, 2-11	Day	Bengeo, SG14 3JA	d73j
Edge Grove	**Boys & Girls, 3-13**	**Day**	**Radlett, WD25 8NL**	e98n
Haberdashers' Boys' School	Boys, 4-18	Day	Elstree, WD6 3AF	h43a
Haberdashers' Girls' School	Girls, 4-18	Day	Elstree, WD6 3BT	h43b
Haileybury	Boys & Girls, 11-18	Day & Boarding	Hertford, SG13 7NU	h97n
Heath Mount School	**Boys & Girls, 2-13**	**Day & Boarding**	**Watton-at-Stone, SG14 3NG**	h93n
Immanuel College	Boys & Girls, 4-18	Day	Bushey, WD23 4EB	i64e
Kingshott School	Boys & Girls, 3-13	Day	Hitchin, SG4 7JX	k17j
Lochinver House School	Boys & Girls, 4-13	Day	Potters Bar, EN6 1LW	l8ll
Lockers Park School	Boys, 4-13	Day & Boarding	Hemel Hempstead, HP1 1TL	l61t
Lyonsdown School	Girls, 3-11	Day	New Barnet, EN5 1SA	l81s
Manor Lodge School	Boys & Girls, 4-11	Day	Shenley, WD7 9BG	m19b
Merchant Taylors' Prep School	Boys, 3-13	Day	Rickmansworth, WD3 1LW	m11l
Mount House School	Boys & Girls, 11-18	Day	Barnet, EN4 ONJ	m0on
Queenswood	Girls, 11-18	Day & Boarding	Hatfield, AL9 6NS	q26n
St Albans High School for Girls	Girls, 4-18	Day	St Albans, AL1 3SJ	s33s
St Albans School	Boys 11-18, Girls 16-18	Day	St Albans, AL3 4HB	s74h
St Christopher School	Boys & Girls, 3-18	Day & Boarding	Letchworth, SG6 3JZ	s83j
St Columba's College	Boys & Girls, 4-18	Day	St Albans, AL3 4AW	s34a
St Edmund's College	**Boys & Girls, 3-18**	**Day & Boarding**	**Ware, SG11 1DS**	s51d
St Francis' College	Girls, 3-18	Day & Boarding	Letchworth Garden City, SG6 3PJ	s43p
St Hilda's School	Girls 2-11, Boys 2-4	Day	Bushey, WD23 3DA	s73d
St Joseph's In The Park	Boys & Girls, 3-11	Day	Hertingfordbury, SG14 2LX	s72l
St Margaret's School	Boys & Girls, 2-18	Day & Boarding	Watford, WD23 1DT	s41d
Stormont School	Girls, 4-11	Day	Potters Bar, EN6 5HA	s75h

Edge Grove — Hertfordshire
Day · Boys & Girls, 3-13 · Radlett, WD25 8NL

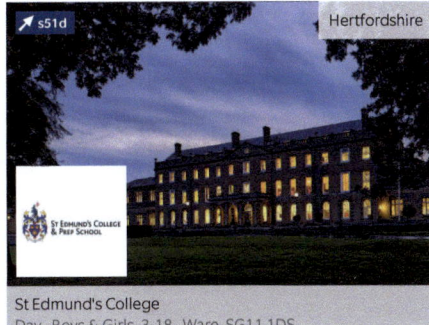

St Edmund's College — Hertfordshire
Day · Boys & Girls, 3-18 · Ware, SG11 1DS

The Purcell School	Boys & Girls, 10-18	Day & Boarding	Bushey, WD23 2TS	t72t
The Royal Masonic School for Girls	Girls, 2-18	Day & Boarding	Rickmansworth, WD3 4HF	t84h
Tring Park for the Performing Arts	Boys & Girls, 7-19	Day & Boarding	Tring, HP23 5LX	t45l
Westbrook Hay Prep School	Boys & Girls, 3-16	Day	Hemel Hempstead, HP1 2RF	w42r
York House School	Boys & Girls, 3-13	Day	Rickmansworth, WD3 4LW	y74l

Norfolk

Beeston Hall School	Boys & Girls, 4-13	Day & Boarding	Cromer, NR27 9NG	b49n
Glebe House School	Boys & Girls, 0-13	Day & Boarding	Hunstanton, PE36 6HW	g66n
Gresham's School	Boys & Girls, 2-18	Day & Boarding	Holt, NR25 6EA	g96e
Langley School	Boys & Girls, 0-18	Day & Boarding	Loddon, NR14 6BJ	l26b
Norwich High School for Girls	Girls, 3-18	Day	Norwich, NR2 2HU	n82h
Norwich School	Boys & Girls, 4-18	Day	Norwich, NR1 4DD	n34d
Thetford Grammar School	Boys & Girls, 3-19	Day & Boarding	Thetford, IP24 3AF	t13a
Town Close School	Boys & Girls, 3-13	Day	Norwich, NR2 2LR	t92l

Suffolk

Barnardiston Hall Prep School	Boys & Girls, 0-13	Day & Boarding	Haverhill, CB9 7TG	b47t
Culford School	Boys & Girls, 1-18	Day & Boarding	Bury St Edmunds, IP28 6TX	c56t
Fairstead House School & Nursery	Boys & Girls, 1-11	Day	Newmarket, CB8 7AA	f97a
Framlingham College	Boys & Girls, 3-18	Day & Boarding	Framlingham, IP13 9EY	f09e
Ipswich High School	Boys & Girls, 3-18	Day & Boarding	Ipswich, IP9 1AZ	i11a
Ipswich School	Boys & Girls, 3-18	Day & Boarding	Ipswich, IP1 3SG	i43s
Old Buckenham Hall School	Boys & Girls, 3-13	Day & Boarding	Ipswich, IP7 7PH	o97p
Orwell Park School	Boys & Girls, 3-13	Day & Boarding	Ipswich, IP10 0ER	o00e
Saint Felix School	Boys & Girls, 2-18	Day & Boarding	Southwold, IP18 6SD	s86s
South Lee School	Boys & Girls, 0-13	Day	Bury St Edmunds, IP33 2BT	s92b
St Joseph's College	Boys & Girls, 3-18	Day & Boarding	Ipswich, IP2 9DR	s29d
The Old School Henstead	Boys & Girls, 2-11	Day	Henstead, NR34 7LG	o67l
The Royal Hospital School	Boys & Girls, 11-18	Day & Boarding	Ipswich, IP9 2RX	t52r
Woodbridge School	Boys & Girls, 4-18	Day & Boarding	Woodbridge, IP12 4JH	w14j

Discover more about schools listed in the Schools' Directory by using the quick link code to jump to the page on our website, e.g. *attain.guide/e98n*

Schools' Directory

Midlands

Use the QR code to learn more about schools in the Midlands

Derbyshire

↗ attain.guide/n86u

Derby Grammar School	Boys & Girls, 4-18	Day	Derby, DE23 4BX	↗ d14b
Derby High School	Boys & Girls, 3-18	Day	Derby, DE23 3DT	↗ d93d
Repton Prep	Boys & Girls, 3-13	Day & Boarding	Milton, DE65 6EJ	↗ r96e
Repton School	Boys & Girls, 13-18	Day & Boarding	Repton, DE65 6FH	↗ r26f
S. Anselm's School	Boys & Girls, 3-13	Day & Boarding	Bakewell, DE45 1DP	↗ s11d
St Peter & St Paul School	Boys & Girls, 4-11	Day	Chesterfield, S41 0EF	↗ s20e

Herefordshire

| Hereford Cathedral School | Boys & Girls, 3-18 | Day & Boarding | Hereford, HR1 2NG | ↗ h62n |

Leicestershire

Leicester Grammar School	Boys & Girls, 3-18	Day	Great Glen, LE8 9FL	↗ l59f
Leicester High School for Girls	Girls, 3-18	Day	Leicester, LE2 2PP	↗ l42p
Loughborough Schools Foundation	Boys & Girls, 0-18	Day & Boarding	Loughborough, LE11 2DU	↗ l12d
Ratcliffe College	Boys & Girls, 3-18	Day & Boarding	Ratcliffe on the Wreake, LE7 4SG	↗ r84s

Lincolnshire

Lincoln Minster School	Boys & Girls, 4-18	Day & Boarding	Lincoln, LN2 5RW	↗ l25r
St Hugh's School, Lincolnshire	Boys & Girls, 2-13	Day & Boarding	Woodhall Spa, LN10 6TQ	↗ s16t
Stamford School	Boys & Girls, 2-18	Day & Boarding	Stamford, PE9 2BQ	↗ s02b
Witham Hall School	Boys & Girls, 4-13	Day & Boarding	Witham-on-the-Hill, PE10 0JJ	↗ w60j

Northamptonshire

Beachborough School	Boys & Girls, 3-13	Day & Boarding	Brackley, NN13 5LB	↗ b05l
Maidwell Hall	Boys & Girls, 4-13	Day & Boarding	Maidwell, NN6 9JG	↗ m39j
Northampton High School	**Girls, 2-18**	**Day**	**Northampton, NN4 6UU**	↗ **n86u**
Oundle School	Boys & Girls, 4-18	Day & Boarding	Peterborough, PE8 4EN	↗ o34e
Pitsford School	Boys & Girls, 3-18	Day	Northampton, NN6 9AX	↗ p19a
Spratton Hall	Boys & Girls, 4-13	Day	Northampton, NN6 8HP	↗ s38h
Wellingborough School	Boys & Girls, 3-18	Day	Wellingborough, NN8 2BX	↗ w72b
Winchester House School	Boys & Girls, 3-13	Day & Boarding	Brackley, NN13 7AZ	↗ w57a

Northampton High School
Day · Girls, 2-18 · Northampton, NN4 6UU

Oakham School
Day · Boys & Girls, 10-18 · Oakham, LE15 6DT

Nottinghamshire

Nottingham Girls' High School	Girls, 4-18	Day	Nottingham, NG1 4JB	↗ n34j
Nottingham High School	Boys & Girls, 4-18	Day	Nottingham, NG7 4ED	↗ n04e
Trent College	Boys & Girls, 0-18	Day & Boarding	Long Eaton, NG10 4AD	↗ t74a
Worksop College	Boys & Girls, 2-18	Day & Boarding	Worksop, S80 3AP	↗ w43a

Rutland

Brooke Priory	Boys & Girls, 2-11	Day	Oakham, LE15 6QW	↗ b46q
Oakham School	**Boys & Girls, 10-18**	**Day & Boarding**	**Oakham, LE15 6DT**	↗ o76d
Uppingham School	Boys & Girls, 13-18	Day & Boarding	Uppingham, LE15 9QE	↗ u29q

Shropshire

Adcote School for Girls	Girls, 7-18	Day & Boarding	Shrewsbury, SY4 2JY	↗ a12j
Bedstone College	Boys & Girls, 3-18	Day & Boarding	Bucknell, SY7 0BG	↗ b30b
Birchfield School	Boys & Girls, 4-16	Day	Wolverhampton, WV7 3AF	↗ b93a
Concord College	Boys & Girls, 13-18	Day & Boarding	Shrewsbury, SY5 7PF	↗ c77p
Ellesmere College	Boys & Girls, 7-18	Day & Boarding	Ellesmere, SY12 9AB	↗ e89a
Moor Park	Boys & Girls, 0-13	Day & Boarding	Ludlow, SY8 4DZ	↗ m44d
Moreton Hall	Boys & Girls, 0-18	Day & Boarding	Oswestry, SY11 3EW	↗ m23e
Oswestry School	Boys & Girls, 4-18	Day & Boarding	Oswestry, SY11 2TL	↗ o32t
Packwood Haugh School	Boys & Girls, 4-13	Day & Boarding	Shrewsbury, SY4 1HX	↗ p91h
Prestfelde	Boys & Girls, 3-13	Day & Boarding	Shrewsbury, SY2 6NZ	↗ p66n
Shrewsbury High School	Girls, 4-18	Day	Shrewsbury, SY1 1TN	↗ s91t
Shrewsbury School	Boys & Girls, 13-18	Day & Boarding	Shrewsbury, SY3 7BA	↗ s57b
The Old Hall School	Boys & Girls, 4-11	Day	Wellington, TF1 3LB	↗ o63l

Schools' Directory

Wrekin College	Boys & Girls, 11-18	Day & Boarding	Telford, TF1 3BH	w23b

Staffordshire

Abbotsholme School	Boys & Girls, 2-18	Day & Boarding	Uttoxeter, ST14 5BS	a75b
Denstone College	Boys & Girls, 4-18	Day & Boarding	Uttoxeter, ST14 5HN	d35h
Lichfield Cathedral School	Boys & Girls, 3-18	Day	Lichfield, WS13 7LH	l67l
Newcastle-under-Lyme School	Boys & Girls, 2-18	Day	Newcastle-under-Lyme, ST5 1DB	n11d
Stafford Grammar School	Boys & Girls, 3-18	Day	Stafford, ST18 9AT	s99a
Yarlet School	Boys & Girls, 2-13	Day & Boarding	Stafford, ST18 9SU	y19s

Warwickshire

Bilton Grange	Boys & Girls, 3-13	Day & Boarding	Rugby, CV22 6QU	b56q
Crackley Hall School	Boys & Girls, 4-11	Day	Kenilworth, CV8 2FT	c92f
Crescent School	Boys & Girls, 4-11	Day	Rugby, CV22 7QH	c47q
King's High Warwick	Girls, 11-18	Day	Warwick, CV34 6YE	k16y
Princethorpe College	Boys & Girls, 11-18	Day	Rugby, CV23 9PX	p39p
Rugby School	Boys & Girls, 11-18	Day & Boarding	Rugby, CV22 5EH	r65e
The Croft Preparatory School	Boys & Girls, 3-11	Day	Stratford-upon-Avon, CV37 7RL	t27r
The Kingsley School	Boys & Girls, 3-18	Day	Leamington Spa, CV32 5RD	t75r
Warwick Preparatory School	Girls 3-11, Boys 3-7	Day	Warwick, CV34 6PL	w96p
Warwick School	Boys, 7-18	Day & Boarding	Warwick, CV34 6PP	w26p

West Midlands

Bablake School	Boys & Girls, 3-18	Day	Coventry, CV1 4AU	b24a
Edgbaston High School for Girls	Girls, 2-18	Day	Edgbaston, B15 3TS	e53t
Elmhurst Ballet School	Boys & Girls, 11-19	Day & Boarding	Edgbaston, B5 7VH	e07v
Eversfield Preparatory School	Boys & Girls, 3-11	Day	Solihull, B91 1AT	e11a
Hallfield School	Boys & Girls, 0-13	Day	Edgbaston, B15 3SJ	h03s
Highclare School	Boys & Girls, 2-18	Day	Erdington, B23 6QL	h96q
King Edward VI High School for Girls	Girls, 11-18	Day	Birmingham, B15 2UB	k62u
King Edward's School	Boys, 11-18	Day	Birmingham, B15 2UA	k32u
King Henry VIII School	Boys & Girls, 3-18	Day	Coventry, CV3 6AQ	k06a
Mayfield Preparatory School	Boys & Girls, 2-11	Day	Walsall, WS1 2PD	m52p
Newbridge Preparatory School	Boys & Girls, 2-11	Day	Wolverhampton, WV6 0LH	n60l
Norfolk House School	Boys & Girls, 3-11	Day	Edgbaston, B15 3PS	n63p

Attain Guide 2025

Ruckleigh School	Boys & Girls, 3-11	Day	Solihull, B91 2AB	r22a
Solihull School	Boys & Girls, 3-18	Day	Solihull, B91 3DJ	s83d
St George's School Edgbaston	Boys & Girls, 3-18	Day	Edgbaston, B15 1RX	s61r
Tettenhall College	Boys & Girls, 2-18	Day & Boarding	Wolverhampton, WV6 8QX	t08q
The Blue Coat School	Boys & Girls, 3-11	Day	Birmingham, B17 0HR	t80h
West House School	Boys 1-11, Girls 1-4	Day	Edgbaston, B15 2NX	w72n
Wolverhampton Grammar School	Boys & Girls, 4-18	Day	Wolverhampton, WV3 9RB	w09r

Worcestershire

Bromsgrove School	**Boys & Girls, 2-18**	**Day & Boarding**	**Bromsgrove, B61 7DU**	**b17d**
Heathfield Knoll School	Boys & Girls, 0-18	Day	Wolverley, DY10 3QE	h33q
King's Hawford	Boys & Girls, 2-11	Day	Worcester, WR3 7SE	k07s
King's St Alban's School	Boys & Girls, 2-11	Day	Worcester, WR1 2NJ	k32n
King's Worcester	Boys & Girls, 11-18	Day	Worcester, WR1 2LL	k72l
Malvern College	Boys & Girls, 13-18	Day & Boarding	Malvern, WR14 3DF	m53d
Malvern St James Girls' School	Girls, 4-18	Day & Boarding	Malvern, WR14 3BA	m23b
RGS Dodderhill	Boys & Girls, 2-11	Day	Droitwich, WR9 0BE	r60b
RGS Springfield	Boys & Girls, 2-11	Day	Worcester, WR1 3DL	r53d
RGS The Grange	Boys & Girls, 2-11	Day	Worcester, WR3 7RR	r77r
RGS Worcester	Boys & Girls, 11-18	Day	Worcester, WR1 1HP	r21h
The Downs Malvern	Boys & Girls, 3-13	Day & Boarding	Malvern, WR13 6EY	t46e
The Elms	Boys & Girls, 3-13	Day & Boarding	Malvern, WR13 6EF	t86e
Winterfold House	Boys & Girls, 0-13	Day	Chaddesley Corbett, DY10 4PW	w04p

Bromsgrove School
Day · Boys & Girls, 2-18 · Bromsgrove, B61 7DU

St Peter's School York
Day · Boys & Girls, 2-18 · York, YO30 6AB

North

Use the QR code to learn more about schools in the North

Cheshire

School	Gender, Ages	Type	Location	Code
Abbey Gate College	Boys & Girls, 4-18	Day	Chester, CH3 6EN	a06e
Alderley Edge School for Girls	Girls, 2-18	Day	Alderley Edge, SK9 7QE	a27q
Cheadle Hulme School	Boys & Girls, 4-18	Day	Cheadle Hulme, SK8 6EF	c86e
Pownall Hall School	Boys & Girls, 2-11	Day	Wilmslow, SK9 5DW	p25d
Stockport Grammar School	Boys & Girls, 3-18	Day	Stockport, SK2 7AF	s97a
Terra Nova School	Boys & Girls, 3-13	Day & Boarding	Holmes Chapel, CW4 8BT	t58b
The Grange School	Boys & Girls, 4-18	Day	Northwich, CW8 1LU	t61l
The Hammond	Boys & Girls, 11-18	Day	Chester, CH2 4ES	t34e
The King's School Chester	Boys & Girls, 4-18	Day	Chester, CH4 7QL	k57q
The King's School Macclesfield	Boys & Girls, 3-18	Day	Macclesfield, SK10 1DA	k61d
The Queen's School Chester	Girls, 4-18	Day	Chester, CH1 2NN	q52n
The Ryleys	Boys & Girls, 1-11	Day	Alderley Edge, SK9 7UY	t57u
Wilmslow Preparatory School	Boys & Girls, 3-11	Day	Wilmslow, SK9 5EG	w95e

County Durham

School	Gender, Ages	Type	Location	Code
Barnard Castle School	Boys & Girls, 4-18	Day & Boarding	Barnard Castle, DL12 8UN	b18u
Durham Cathedral Schools	Boys & Girls, 3-18	Day & Boarding	Durham, DH1 4SZ	d24s
Durham High School for Girls	Girls, 3-18	Day	Durham, DH1 3TB	d93t

Cumbria

School	Gender, Ages	Type	Location	Code
Austin Friars School	Boys & Girls, 3-18	Day	Carlisle, CA3 9PB	a29p
Hunter Hall Preparatory School	Boys & Girls, 3-11	Day	Penrith, CA11 8UA	h28u
Sedbergh School	Boys & Girls, 0-18	Day & Boarding	Sedbergh, LA10 5HG	s35h
Windermere School	Boys & Girls, 3-18	Day & Boarding	Windermere, LA23 1NW	w71n

Discover more about schools listed in the Schools' Directory by using the quick link code to jump to the page on our website, e.g. *attain.guide/s26a*

Attain Guide 2025

Greater Manchester

Altrincham Prep School	Boys & Girls, 2-11	Day	Bowden, WA14 2RR	a22r
Bolton School	**Boys & Girls, 0-18**	**Day**	**Bolton, BL1 4PA**	b84p
Bury Grammar School	Boys & Girls, 3-18	Day	Bury, BL9 0HN	b20h
Chetham's School of Music	Boys & Girls, 8-18	Day & Boarding	Long Millgate, M3 1SB	c31s
Manchester High School for Girls	Girls, 4-18	Day	Grangethorpe Road, M14 6HS	m16h
St Ambrose Preparatory School	Boys & Girls, 3-11	Day	Altrincham, WA15 0HF	s40h
St Bede's College	Boys & Girls, 3-18	Day	Manchester, M16 8HX	s28h
The Manchester Grammar School	Boys, 7-18	Day	Old Hall Lane, M13 0XT	m20x
Withington Girls' School	**Girls, 7-18**	**Day**	**Manchester, M14 6BL**	w16b

Lancashire

AKS Lytham	Boys & Girls, 0-18	Day	Lytham St Annes, FY8 1DT	a01d
Ashbridge School and Nursery	Boys & Girls, 0-11	Day	Preston, PR4 4AQ	a04a
Kirkham Grammar School	Boys & Girls, 3-18	Day & Boarding	Kirkham, PR4 2BH	k22b
Rossall School	Boys & Girls, 0-18	Day & Boarding	Fleetwood, FY7 8JW	r88j
St Pius X Preparatory School	Boys & Girls, 2-11	Day	Preston, PR2 8RD	s98r
Stonyhurst College	Boys & Girls, 3-18	Day & Boarding	Clitheroe, BB7 9PZ	s69p
Westholme School	Boys & Girls, 4-18	Day	Blackburn, BB2 6QU	w16q

Merseyside

Birkenhead School	Boys & Girls, 0-18	Day	Birkenhead, CH43 2JD	b52j
Merchant Taylors' School Crosby	Boys & Girls, 4-18	Day	Crosby, L23 0QP	m30q
St Mary's College	Boys & Girls, 0-18	Day	Crosby, L23 5TW	s75t
The Belvedere Preparatory School	Boys & Girls, 3-11	Day	Liverpool, L8 3TF	b73t

Northumberland

Longridge Towers School	Boys & Girls, 3-18	Day & Boarding	Berwick-upon-Tweed, TD15 2XQ	l62x
Mowden Hall School	Boys & Girls, 3-13	Day & Boarding	Stocksfield, NE43 7TP	m87t

Tyne & Wear

Dame Allan's Schools	Boys & Girls, 3-18	Day	Newcastle upon Tyne, NE4 9YJ	d49y
Newcastle High School for Girls	Girls, 3-18	Day	Newcastle upon Tyne, NE2 3BA	n13b
Newcastle Preparatory School	Boys & Girls, 3-11	Day	Newcastle upon Tyne, NE2 4RH	n14r
Newcastle School for Boys	Boys, 3-18	Day	Newcastle upon Tyne, NE3 4ES	n64e

Schools' Directory

Royal Grammar School Newcastle	Boys & Girls, 7-18	Day	Newcastle upon Tyne, NE2 4DX	r54d
Teesside High School	Boys & Girls, 3-18	Day	Stockton-on-Tees, TS16 9AT	t19a
Westfield School	Girls, 3-18	Day	Newcastle upon Tyne, NE3 4HS	w34h

Yorkshire

Ackworth School	Boys & Girls, 3-18	Day & Boarding	Pontefract, WF7 7LT	a67l
Ashville College	Boys & Girls, 2-18	Day & Boarding	Harrogate, HG2 9JP	a69j
Aysgarth School	Boys & Girls, 3-13	Day & Boarding	Bedale, DL8 1TF	a91t
Belmont Grosvenor School	Boys & Girls, 3-11	Day	Harrogate, HG3 2JG	b32j
Birkdale School	Boys & Girls, 4-18	Day	Sheffield, S10 3DH	b23d
Bootham School	Boys & Girls, 3-18	Day & Boarding	York, YO30 7BU	b37b
Bradford Grammar School	Boys & Girls, 4-18	Day	Bradford, BD9 4JP	b74j
Fulneck School	Boys & Girls, 3-18	Day & Boarding	Pudsey, LS28 8DS	f38d
Gateways School	Boys & Girls, 2-18	Day	Leeds, LS17 9LE	g19l
Giggleswick School	Boys & Girls, 2-18	Day & Boarding	Settle, BD24 0DE	g50d
Harrogate Ladies' College	Girls 2-18, Boys 2-11	Day & Boarding	Harrogate, HG1 2QG	h62q
Hill House School	Boys & Girls, 3-18	Day	Doncaster, DN9 3GG	h73g
Hymers College	Boys & Girls, 3-18	Day	Hull, HU3 1LW	h91l
Moorfield School	Boys & Girls, 2-11	Day	Ilkley, LS29 8RL	m28r
Moorlands School	Boys & Girls, 2-11	Day	Leeds, LS16 5PF	m85p
Mount St Mary's College	Boys & Girls, 3-18	Day & Boarding	Sheffield, S21 3YL	m73y
Pocklington School	Boys & Girls, 3-18	Day & Boarding	Pocklington, YO42 2NH	p42n
Queen Ethelburga's College	Boys & Girls, 0-18	Day & Boarding	York, YO26 9SS	q79s
Queen Margaret's	Girls, 11-18	Day & Boarding	Escrick, YO19 6EU	q96e
Queen Mary's School	Girls 4-16, Boys 4-7	Day & Boarding	Thirsk, YO7 3BZ	q13b
Read School	Boys & Girls, 4-18	Day & Boarding	Selby, YO8 8NL	r98n
Richmond House School	Boys & Girls, 3-11	Day	Leeds, LS16 5LG	r15l
Rishworth School	Boys & Girls, 3-18	Day & Boarding	Rishworth, HX6 4QA	r64q
Scarborough College	Boys & Girls, 3-18	Day & Boarding	Scarborough, YO11 3BA	s23b
Sheffield Girls'	Girls, 4-18	Day	Sheffield, S10 2PE	s02p
Silcoates School	Boys & Girls, 3-18	Day	Wakefield, WF2 0PD	s70p
St Peter's School York	**Boys & Girls, 2-18**	**Day & Boarding**	**York, YO30 6AB**	s26a
Terrington Hall School	Boys & Girls, 3-13	Day & Boarding	York, YO60 6PR	t56p
The Froebelian School	Boys & Girls, 3-11	Day	Horsforth, LS18 4LB	t24l
The Gleddings Preparatory School	Boys & Girls, 3-11	Day	Halifax, HX3 0JB	t90j

The Grammar School at Leeds	Boys & Girls, 3-18	Day	Alwoodley, LS17 8GS	t98g
The Mount School Huddersfield	Boys & Girls, 3-11	Day	Edgerton, HD2 2AP	t72a
The Mount School York	Girls, 3-18	Day & Boarding	York, YO24 4DD	t34d
Tranby	Boys & Girls, 3-18	Day	Hull, HU10 7EH	t47e
Wakefield Grammar Foundation	Boys & Girls, 3-18	Day	Wakefield, WF1 3UF	w83u
Westbourne School	Boys & Girls, 3-16	Day	Sheffield, S10 2QT	w02q
Woodhouse Grove School	Boys & Girls, 3-18	Day & Boarding	Apperley Bridge, BD10 0NR	w40n
Yarm School	Boys & Girls, 3-18	Day	Yarm, TS15 9EJ	y69e

Rest of the UK

Use the QR code to learn more about schools in the rest of the UK

Scotland

Albyn School	Boys & Girls, 2-18	Day	Aberdeen, AB15 4PB	a14p
Ardvreck School	Boys & Girls, 3-13	Day & Boarding	Crieff, PH7 4EX	a04e
Belhaven Hill School	Boys & Girls, 5-13	Day & Boarding	East Lothian, EH42 1NN	b21n
Cargilfield Preparatory School	Boys & Girls, 3-13	Day & Boarding	Edinburgh, EH4 6HU	c66h
Craigclowan Preparatory School	Boys & Girls, 3-13	Day	Perth, PH2 8PS	c28p
Dollar Academy	Boys & Girls, 5-18	Day & Boarding	Clackmannanshire, FK14 7DU	d27d
ESMS Junior School	Boys & Girls, 3-11	Day	Edinburgh, EH4 3EZ	e93e
Fettes College	Boys & Girls, 7-18	Day & Boarding	Edinburgh, EH4 1QX	f51q
George Heriot's School	Boys & Girls, 4-18	Day	Edinburgh, EH3 9EQ	g29e
George Watson's College	Boys & Girls, 3-18	Day	Edinburgh, EH10 5EG	g95e
Glenalmond College	Boys & Girls, 12-18	Day & Boarding	Perth, PH1 3RY	g63r
Gordonstoun School	Boys & Girls, 4-18	Day & Boarding	Moray, IV30 5RF	g05r
High School of Dundee	Boys & Girls, 5-18	Day	Dundee, DD1 1HU	h41h
High School of Glasgow	Boys & Girls, 3-18	Day	Glasgow, G13 1PL	h71p
Hutchesons' Grammar School	Boys & Girls, 5-18	Day	Glasgow, G41 4NW	h14n
Kelvinside Academy	Boys & Girls, 3-18	Day	Glasgow, G12 0SW	k60s
Kilgraston School	Girls 5-18, Boys 5-12	Day & Boarding	Perthshire, PH2 9BQ	k29b
Lomond School	Boys & Girls, 3-18	Day & Boarding	Argyll & Bute, G84 9JX	l29j
Loretto School	Boys & Girls, 3-18	Day & Boarding	East Lothian, EH21 7RE	l17r
Merchiston Castle School	Boys, 7-18	Day & Boarding	Edinburgh, EH13 0PU	m90p
Morrison's Academy	Boys & Girls, 2-18	Day	Crieff, PH7 3AN	m63a
Robert Gordon's College	Boys & Girls, 3-18	Day	Aberdeen, AB10 1FE	r91f

Schools' Directory

School	Type	Mode	Location	Code
St Aloysius' College	Boys & Girls, 3-18	Day	Glasgow, G3 6RJ	s26r
St Columba's School	Boys & Girls, 3-18	Day	Inverclyde, PA13 4AU	s54a
St George's, Edinburgh	Girls, 3-18	Day & Boarding	Edinburgh, EH12 6BG	s06b
St Leonards School	Boys & Girls, 5-18	Day & Boarding	St Andrews, KY16 9QJ	s19q
St Margaret's School for Girls	Girls 3-18, Boys 3-5	Day	Aberdeen, AB10 1RU	s41r
St Mary's School Melrose	Boys & Girls, 2-13	Day & Boarding	Melrose, TD6 9LN	s79l
Stewart's Melville College	Boys & Girls, 12-18	Day & Boarding	Edinburgh, EH4 3EZ	s93e
Strathallan School	Boys & Girls, 7-18	Day & Boarding	Perth, PH2 9EG	s89e
The Edinburgh Academy	Boys & Girls, 2-18	Day	Edinburgh, EH3 5BL	t45b
The Glasgow Academy	Boys & Girls, 3-18	Day	Glasgow, G13 1PL	t51p
The Mary Erskine School	Girls, 12-18	Day & Boarding	Edinburgh, EH4 3NT	t03n

Wales

Cathedral School Llandaff	Boys & Girls, 3-18	Day	Cardiff, CF5 2YH	c42y
Christ College Brecon	Boys & Girls, 4-18	Day & Boarding	Powys, LD3 8AG	c18a
Dean Close St John's	Boys & Girls, 1-13	Day & Boarding	Chepstow, NP16 7LE	d77l
Haberdashers' Monmouth Schools	**Boys & Girls, 3-18**	**Day & Boarding**	**Monmouth, NP25 3HG**	h63h
Howell's School, Llandaff	Girls, 3-18	Day	Cardiff, CF5 2YD	h52y
Llandovery College	Boys & Girls, 4-18	Day & Boarding	Carmarthenshire, SA20 0EE	l70e
Myddelton College	Boys & Girls, 4-18	Day & Boarding	Denbigh, LL16 3EN	m53e
Rougemont School	Boys & Girls, 3-18	Day	Newport, NP20 6QB	r66q
Ruthin School	Boys & Girls, 11-18	Day & Boarding	Ruthin, LL15 1EE	r81e
Rydal Penrhos	Boys & Girls, 2-18	Day & Boarding	Clwyd, LL29 7BT	r27b
St David's College	Boys & Girls, 9-18	Day & Boarding	Llandudno, LL30 1RD	s91r
St John's College Cardiff	Boys & Girls, 3-18	Day	Cardiff, CF3 5YX	s05y

Northern Ireland

Belfast Royal Academy	Boys & Girls, 3-18	Day	Belfast, BT14 6JL	b66j
Campbell College	Boys & Girls, 3-18	Day & Boarding	Belfast, BT4 2ND	c82n
Coleraine Grammar School	Boys & Girls, 11-18	Day	Coleraine, BT51 3LA	c33l
Royal Belfast Academical Institution	Boys, 3-18	Day	Belfast, BT1 6DL	r76d
The Royal School Armagh	Boys & Girls, 11-18	Day & Boarding	Armagh, BT61 9DH	r39d
The Royal School Dungannon	Boys & Girls, 11-18	Day & Boarding	Dungannon, BT71 6EG	r06e

References

Quotes were included from the following articles from back issues of Attain:
(1) Hands, Dr Tim: 'New beginnings', Attain (2016); (2) Skrine, Helen: 'Is your child really happy?', Attain (2016); (3) Tait, Peter: 'The Years that Count', Attain (2013); (4) Trafford, Dr Bernard: 'The Power of Gravitas', Attain (2015); (5) Tait, Peter: 'Why the early years matter', Attain (2016); (6) Hands, Dr Tim: 'The truth behind league tables', Attain (2016); (7) Tait, Peter: 'Parents Under Pressure', Attain (2015); (8) Robinson, Julie: 'Why independent schools are different', Attain (2016); (9) Hands, Dr Tim: 'Scholarships be damned', Attain (2015); (10) Tait, Peter: 'Ten Parental Observations', Attain (2015).

Photo Credits

iStock.com/RichVintage (cover, p2, p6, p10, p13, p17, p25, p37, p41, p45, p49, p66), iStock.com/monkeybusinessimages (p21), iStock.com/Marilyn Nieves (p29), iStock.com/Matt_Brown (p33), iStock.com/Choreograph (p53), iStock.com/Kenishirotie (p56), iStock.com/pinstock (p59), iStock.com/shironosov (p63), Sydenham High/Tom Soper (p72), Wycombe Abbey/David Levenson (p78), Bournemouth Collegiate School/Millie Pilkington (p89), Sandroyd School/Millie Pilkington (p91), St Mary's School, Cambridge/Chris Reeve (p93), Beechwood Park/Navy Studios (p94), Edge Grove/Adam Scott (p95), St Edmund's College/Chris Reeve (p95). The publishers have attempted to acknowledge all known copyright holders of photographs included in this book but would be pleased to correct any omissions in future editions.